CLANS & TARTANS

CLANS & TARTANS

JAMES MACKAY

THUNDER BAY
P·R·E·S·S

San Diego, California

Thunder Bay Press

An imprint of the Advantage Publishers Group

5880 Oberlin Drive, San Diego, CA 92121-4794

www.thunderbaybooks.com

Produced by PRC Publishing Ltd.

64 Brewery Road, London N7 9NT, U.K.

© 2002 PRC Publishing Ltd.

A member of **Chrysalis** Books plc

Library of Congress Cataloging-in-Publication Data:

Mackay, Jame A. (James Alexander), 1936–

    Clans & Tartans / James Mackay.

        p. cm.

    Includes index.

    ISBN 1-57145-980-4

    1. Clans–Scotland. 2. Tartans–Scotland.

    3. Scotland–Genealogy. I. Title: Clans and tartans. II. Title.

    DA880.H76M28 2003

    929'.2'09411--dc21   2002075690

Printed and bound in Malaysia

1 2 3 4 5   07 06 05 04 03

ACKNOWLEDGMENTS

The publisher wishes to thank all those who kindly supplied images for this book. All tartan images were supplied by the Scottish Tartans Society, including that on the cover, with the following exceptions:

The Ayrshire District tartan (page 28) is a registered design and should not be reproduced without the copyright holder's permission, namely Philip Smith.

The image of the Black Watch tartan (page 33) was kindly supplied by the Scottish Tartans Authority.

The St. Columba image (page 205) was kindly supplied by Peter MacDonald and should not be reproduced without the copyright holder's permission. The design is protected by Registered Design No. 602274 and is available from:

Peter MacDonald

Tartan Design & Consultancy

Crieff

Perthshire

UK

www.scottishtartans.co.uk

The designs of the following tartans are protected by copyright and should not be reproduced without the permission of the copyright holder, MacNaughton Holdings Limited:

Antrim, Armagh, Carlow, Cavan, Cork, Donegal, Down, Dublin, Fermanagh, Galway, Irish National, Kildare, Kilkenny, Laois, Limerick, Londonderry, Mayo, Roscommon, Stone of Destiny, Tipperary, Tyrone, Waterford, Westmeath, Wexford, Wicklow.

Special thanks to Brian Wilton of the Scottish Tartans Authority (www.tartansauthority.com) for his help with this book.

Contents

Introduction

The notion of people belonging to a family or a tribe, or even an entire race being the children of a common ancestor, is to be found all over the world (as in, for instance, the Jews regarding themselves as the children of Israel). The word "clan" in its original sense referred to a kindred group. Celtic society was organized on family lines that were reflected in laws, customs, and systems of landholding. The Welsh word *plant*, meaning "seed" (from the Latin *planta*) became transformed in Goidelic (Q-Celtic) as *cland*, from which comes the Gaelic word *clann*, originally meaning "seed" but since acquiring its modern meaning of "children." Traces of these may be found in many countries, wherever Celtic tribes left their mark in their westward migration across central Europe in pre-Christian times. Vestiges of this ancient system survived in the remotest parts of the continent, on the western fringes of the British Isles, in Wales, Ireland, and the Highlands of Scotland.

In Ireland the head of a family would adopt the word *Ua* (grandson), followed by the name of an ancestor, as in "Ua Suilleabhain," which became anglicized as "O'Sullivan." The chief would simply be known by that name, while his followers would take it as a surname after their chosen forenames. In Scotland, Wales, and also in Ireland, surnames were originally formed simply by adding details of a person's father, and sometimes their grandfather as well. For example, "James, the son of John, son of Donald" was known in

Right: A young girl performs Highland dancing in traditional dress.

Gaelic. as "Seumas mac Iain mhic Domhnuill." In the case of a woman, "Mary, the daughter of John, son of Donald" would be "Mairi nighean Iain mhic Domhnuill," though as a rule the word *nighean* (daughter) was shortened in surnames to *nic*.

In the anglicized forms of Highland surnames, "Mac" is used for both sexes, but in Gaelic, female surnames often begin with "Nic." It should be noted that in Welsh (P-Celtic), the word for "son" was rendered as *map*, but the initial consonant disappeared, so surnames developed as "Ap," as in Ap Rhys (son of Rhys), anglicized as Price or Preece. In Manx (Q-Celtic), "Mac" likewise became eroded, leaving only the final consonant, rendered as "C," "K," or "Qu," as in Clucas (son of Lucas), Kermode (son of Dermot or Diarmid), and Quilliam (son of William).

The gradual adoption of surnames in Scotland in the thirteenth and fourteenth centuries developed the idea that all persons who bore a particular surname were somehow related through some common ancestor, hence the emphasis on the word *clann*. The word *siol* (seed) was also used, either to denote a division in a large clan or a confederation of clans that trace their descent from a common ancestor.

In its purest form, the clan was essentially a family group whose members traced their roots back to a common ancestor and who were therefore linked by blood ties. It included all illegitimate children—so long as their fathers acknowledged paternity—as well as children adopted or fostered by the family. It might also include the children of women who had married outside the family group and who therefore bore a different surname. More commonly, however, the appearance of other surnames within the clan arose as a result of landless men or outlaws attaching themselves to the clan for protection, rendering service in return. From this arose the notion of the *sept*. This word, derived from the Latin *septum*, a fence or enclosure, alludes to the fact that originally a certain piece of clan land was set aside for these landless followers, where they could establish a village of their own. Rather confusingly, the Gaelic word for a sept is *fine*, often used indiscriminately to denote a clan, tribe, or kindred. In Ireland, "Fine Gael" is the name of one of the major political parties. Over the centuries certain surnames have become widely accepted as septs of clans, although in some cases such surnames may be septs of two or more clans just as, conversely, a clan may have different septs.

Although the clan system in Scotland was smashed in the aftermath of the Jacobite Rebellion of 1745–46, the age-old allegiance of the clansman to his chief was gradually replaced by the ties of kindred, in which the possession of a common surname became of paramount importance. A surname provides a feeling of solidarity that today links people from every part of the globe and every walk of life. The spread of Scottish clan names to every

INTRODUCTION

part of the world is a reflection of the Scottish diaspora. It has been estimated that there are over thirty million people outside Scotland who are of Scottish descent—six times the number of people actually residing in Scotland.

Possession of a Scottish surname entitles you to wear the tartan of your clan. Even if your surname is not among one of the hundred or so great clans, the chances are that you bear the surname of one of the numerous septs. In relatively recent years, the notion has arisen that, in default of a clan or sept surname, you can wear the tartan of your mother's (or grandmother's) clan. Purists argue against this widespread practice, pointing out that there are perfectly good alternatives. A subject of Her Majesty the Queen of England, for example, could wear a Royal Stewart tartan to show their allegiance, or the Caledonia tartan, cunningly devised in the nineteenth century to embrace all people of Scotland, or even the Jacobite tartan, allegedly worn by the clanless followers of Bonnie Prince Charlie. There are even occupational tartans designed to be worn by shepherds or ministers of religion, and if all else fails, there is the Burns check (invented by a Frenchman and designed to be worn by fans of the poet Robert Burns).

Clan names appear in the unlikeliest of places. There are many Americans of Afro-Caribbean origin who are the bearers of Scottish surnames, derived from the days of slavery when slaves took the names of their owners or plantation overseers, or as a result of liaisons between masters and their female slaves. The same applies to many people in Bermuda, the Bahamas, and the West Indian islands.

There are also many Scottish names to be found throughout the Pacific Islands and Southeast Asia, arising no doubt from miscegenation, the mixed marriages of Scottish traders and officials with local women. A surprisingly large number of Mac names will also be found in the telephone directories of every European country. In some cases, this arises from the tremendous movement of population, especially within the European Community, in recent years. In many others, however, it goes back to the Thirty Years' War (1618–48), when thousands of Highlanders were recruited by Gustavas Vasa, while many others entered the Garde d'Ecosse and other units in the French or Austrian service. After many years of campaigning in every part of Europe, Scots often married and settled down, adding their surnames to the local population. The Mackays of Holland retained their surname (the clan chief eventually became a member of the Dutch peerage), but elsewhere they became the Von Keys of Sweden and the Makkais of Hungary.

While many people in Russia with the surname of Gordon may well be descended from Patrick Gordon of Auchleries (1635–99), who rose to the highest rank in the Russian army under Peter the Great, they are more likely

to be Jews deriving their surname from Grodno. Similarly, Grant and Morrison are often Jewish surnames without any connection to the Scottish clans of the same name.

The Clan System

Few people in Scotland can trace their roots with any certainty back before the beginning of the eighteenth century because parish records seldom exist from the period before then. On the other hand, clan histories often go back into the very mists of antiquity. Even if a personal link cannot be established, kinship may be claimed, on the strength of a surname alone, with people who existed a thousand years ago, and in some cases even further back in time.

Clan histories and genealogies (like the gaily colored tartans themselves) are largely a product of the late eighteenth and early nineteenth centuries. Some far-fetched claims later gave rise to a measure of healthy

skepticism regarding these long pedigrees, but a more scholarly approach in recent years, coupled with a systematic study of the vast body of documentary material of all kinds, has served to redress the balance. Two facts are indisputable: Celtic society was organized on tribal lines and the population of Scotland a thousand years ago was very small and often isolated. The popular notion that the Picts somehow died out soon after they merged with the Scots has now been shown to be quite erroneous, not only in the survival of place-names and artifacts, but also in the racial characteristics that are still prevalent in the Highlands. The Picts (from Latin *Picti*, the painted ones) were the oldest established Celtic inhabitants of what is now Scotland, the tribes known to the Romans as the

Above: Eilean Donan Castle on Loch Duich, Dornie, Scotland

Caledonii and Maeatae. The Scots (Scotti) were migrants from northern Ireland who settled in Argyll in the early sixth century and established the kingdom of Dalriada under Fergus Mac Erc and his brothers Lorn and Angus, from whom came two of the oldest territorial divisions as well as tribal names.

Descent in the Picts was matrilineal, so when Alpin, King of Scots, married a Pictish princess, their son Kenneth fell heir to both kingdoms and in 843 became King of the Picts and Scots, merging the Q-Celtic elements in the lands to the north of the Forth-Clyde isthmus. Southwest Scotland was occupied by the Britons of Strathclyde (P-Celtic, speaking a language akin to Welsh), while the southeast was settled by Anglo-Saxon peoples. Other disparate groups were the Attacotti of Galloway, who retained their individuality until the fifteenth century, and Norse settlements in the far north as well as the islands. Add the Norman mercenaries recruited by King David in the early twelfth century and the European merchants and traders, whose descendants rejoice in such surnames as Fleming (from Flanders), Bremner (from Bremen), and Imrie (from Hungary), and it will be seen that the Scots of the past were very mixed—to say nothing of the present day.

Although the clan system of land tenure was established in the Celtic parts of Scotland by the sixth century, if not earlier, the present structure of clans, with identifiable surnames, arose very much later. It was beginning to emerge in the twelfth century and was well established by the 1400s, although in many cases clans trace their origins back to a much earlier (and perhaps mythical) ancestor. Pictland was divided into seven great tribal provinces: Caith (Caithness and Sutherland), Ce (Mar and Buchan), Ciric (the Mearns), Fibh (Fife), Fidach (Ross and Moray), Fodhla (Atholl), and Fortrenn (western Perthshire). The historian Skene asserted that the basic tribal unit was the *tuath*, several of which formed a *mortuath* (great tribe). Two or more mortuaths formed a *coicidh* (province), which was ruled by a *righ* (from Latin *rex*, a king). These provinces were delineated in such a way that they converged at a central point where the *Ard-Righ* (high king) had his capital at Scone in Perthshire. The Scots added their tribal districts of Dalriada and together these divisions produced the later clan lands as well as the counties of more modern times. By the twelfth century there was only one righ, but under him the head of the tuath was the *toiseach* (a term used in the Republic of Ireland to denote the prime minister), while the head of the mortuath was the *mormaer* (great steward).

The clan system was a peculiarly Scottish compromise between the age-old tribal organization and the concepts of feudalism introduced by Margaret, the Anglo-Saxon princess who became the wife of King Malcolm Canmore. This system was considerably refined and expanded by their sons, with the aid of Norman mercenaries and administrators in the twelfth century. The clans that emerged were generally subdivisions of the earlier tribes, confined to a particular island, strath, or glen. Over the ensuing centuries, there was a great deal of feuding and fighting, and some clans became much larger and more powerful than their neighbors. Attempts by successive monarchs to curb the power of the great clans included the occasional punitive expedition, but more often than not chiefs were bought off with grants of land and titles. By an Act of the Scottish Parliament in 1587, measures were taken for the pacification of the Highlands, Islands, and Borders. Associated with this is the earliest attempt to enumerate the various clans, their chiefs, chieftains, captains, tanists, and other officials, as well as recognition of the fact that clansmen owed their first allegiance to their chiefs. The chief had the power of life and death over his clansmen, but his autocracy was tempered by certain democratic safeguards. He could only make war on another clan with the consent of the whole clan, and he administered the clan lands for the good of all, with an elaborate system of rules along communistic lines.

The chief's ability to mobilize his clansmen was both his strength and ultimately his undoing. Charles II cynically harnessed this powerful warrior class to terrorize the Lowlands into accepting his religious policies. Memories of the depredations of the Highland Host of 1678 remained

long and bitter, and help to explain the way in which the country tended to polarize at the time of the Revolution in 1688–90 and again during the Jacobite rebellions of 1715, 1719, and 1745–46. There were clans that supported the House of Orange or the Hanoverian dynasty. The massacre of the MacDonalds of Glencoe by the Campbells in 1692 is a prime example of this, just as there were probably as many Highlanders in the army of the Duke of Cumberland at Culloden as in the Jacobite forces ranged against them.

But Prince Charles Edward Stuart had derived his strength from the clans and a vengeful government decided that they must be crushed for all time. The power of the chiefs was destroyed by the abolition of heritable jurisdictions in 1747 but those symbols, which made the Highlander different from the Lowlander, had also to be eradicated. The wearing of tartan was outlawed in 1746 and Highlanders were compelled to swear an oath that they would give up their Highland garb just as assuredly as they were forced to give up their weapons. Not until 1782 was this legislation revoked, but by that time the Highlander had proved his worth as a soldier in the service of the Crown, the Highland regiments offering the only legitimate outlet for wearing tartan.

The Act of 1747 transformed the clan chief into a landowner. Instead of holding the clan lands in trust, he now became the landlord. In the next generation, many

Scotsmen in traditional dress for the Highland Games take a break with a glass of whisky.

chiefs gravitated toward Edinburgh and then London, content to live off their rents and leave the management of their estates in the hands of tacksmen and factors. In the 1780s, the ruthless process of removing clansmen from the straths and glens began. This was done to make way for blackface sheep, and when even they proved uneconomical, vast tracts of the Highlands were converted into deer forests for the sport of wealthy Lowlanders and Sassenachs. The Highland clearances lasted, off and on, for a hundred years. In the course of the nineteenth century, and especially in the decades after Waterloo (1815), thousands of embittered clansmen and their families emigrated to North America, Australia, New Zealand, Patagonia, and Natal. Not until the 1880s, when a royal commission was set up to inquire into conditions in the crofting counties, was this process halted, but by that time it was too late. Today the once-silent glens have come to life again, peopled by incomers from the south, from England and even Europe, escaping the rat race, but sometimes by expatriate Scots rediscovering their roots.

Tartan

"The garb of old Gaul" consisted of a piece of woolen cloth, about 6½ feet in width and up to 20 feet in length, carefully gathered into pleats at the center, one end wound around the wearer's back, over the shoulder, and secured by a brooch. A stout leather belt secured the garment at the waist and the lower part was pleated and gathered to form the *feileadh beag*, or "little kilt." From the lower part of this garment developed the *philabeg*, or kilt as we know it today, although in its present form it is largely an invention of the eighteenth century.

The origins of the distinctive cloth patterns, which are collectively known as "tartan," are shrouded in controversy. To the Gael it was *breacan feile* (speckled cloth) but the word "tartan" appears to come from the French *tirtaine*, implying a European origin. The earliest written references to tartan occur in the accounts of the treasurer of James III in 1471. References to tartan in Gaelic literature date from

the early sixteenth century, and descriptions of the multicolored cloth appear in Lowland Scots by the 1570s. Martin Martin, writing a century later, commented on the fact that the *sett* (pattern) varied from place to place, so that a person might identify the origins of the wearer from the colors of his cloth. From this it appears that the earliest tartans were territorial rather than clan-based, although in many cases the two would have been synonymous.

The cloth itself was woven and then dyed in a pattern of checks that depended largely on the pigments available locally. The muted greens and russet hues were derived from mosses, lichens, plants, and berries, and imported indigo supplied the deep blue shades. The oldest tartans tend to be the darkest and it was the dark blue and green check worn by the government troops policing the Highlands that gave rise to the name of the Black Watch. From this "Government tartan," as it was officially styled, developed many of the other tartans worn by the Highland regiments, varied by the inclusion of contrasting stripes of white, yellow, or red.

The Government tartan with a yellow stripe was worn by the Gordon Highlanders, and became the Gordon tartan, while the same tartan, but with stripes of white and red at right angles, was worn by the Seaforth Highlanders and became the tartan of the MacKenzies. Other clans whose tartans are similar to the Government tartan include Campbell, Mackay, and Sutherland, while Forbes,

Gordon, Lamont, MacKinlay, and Murray tartans have it as a basis on which counterstripes of contrasting colors have also been added.

Most of the tartans as we know them today date back no further than the 1820s as a result of two disparate factors. The first was the enterprising firm of William Wilson of Bannockburn, which held the contract to supply tartan cloth to the Highland regiments at home and abroad. The second was the visit of King George IV to Scotland in 1822, the first visit north of the Border of the reigning monarch since the time of Charles II. Sir Walter Scott, who stage-managed this event, persuaded the portly monarch to don a kilt, complete with flesh-colored tights. Although the resulting spectacle must have been quite ludicrous, it triggered off a craze for tartan that has endured to this day. It went hand in hand with the romanticism of the Highlands (later fueled by Queen Victoria and Prince Albert) and created a demand for tartans distinctive to every clan, sept, and even the great families of the Borders, which had never worn tartan in historical times. Today each of the hundred-odd clans of Scotland, together with most of their septs, have their own setts; but in many cases variety is imparted by the invention of "ancient" (based on original patterns), "hunting" (muted shades for deer-stalking) and "dress" (suitably flamboyant for evening wear), as well as ordinary tartans for day wear, so that the number of tartans now runs to many hundreds.

Tartan has developed a heraldry of its own; but even if the colors are not as readily symbolic as the devices on armorial bearings, they are instantly recognizable and identify the wearer's clan. Today, tartan has become universal, though sometimes with surprising results. The late Professor Toshio Namba of Tokyo, a Burns scholar of world rank, discovered that his name translated into English as "son of Tosh" and for this reason habitually wore a Mackintosh kilt when attending Robert Burns conferences.

There are hardy souls who are never seen in trousers. In all weather, they wear the kilt and some may do so without underwear in the traditional manner. For most people, however, the kilt is reserved for special occasions such as Robert Burns's birthday (January 25), St. Andrew's Day (November 30), clan gatherings, and Highland Games. These four events are now worldwide and some of the largest parades of tartan are to be seen at such spectacular gatherings as the Grandfather Mountain Highland Games in Georgia and the Glengarry Highland Games in Ontario, although there is nothing to beat the

Right: Edinburgh Castle, Scotland

Braemar Gathering (attended by the Royal Family from nearby Balmoral) or the Cowal Games for the authentic flavor of piping contests, caber-tossing, hammer-throwing, Highland dancing and, of course, people-watching.

The Future of Tartan

There has been a remarkable explosion of tartan within the past few years, resulting both in an enormous increase in the number of different patterns and in the uses to which it is put. In 1831, James Logan recorded a mere fifty-five tartans in his book *The Scottish Gael*. By 1906, when William and A. K. Johnston of Edinburgh published a guide to tartans, the number had doubled. Undoubtedly, what gave tartan its greatest boost was the interest taken in all things Highland by Queen Victoria, but the ball was set rolling by two remarkable Englishmen with the distinctly non-Scottish surname of Allen. Having settled in Scotland in the 1830s, however, they proceeded to become more Scottish than the Scots, changing their name successively to Allan, Hay Allan and then, quite unashamedly, Stuart, with the distinguished forenames of John Sobieski and Charles Edward. This reinforced their claim to be descended from the Old Pretender (James III) and his wife Clementina Sobieska, granddaughter of the celebrated Polish King Jan Sobieski. The Sobieski Stuarts, as this pair

of con men came to be known, profited for a time from a resurgence of Jacobite sentiment before they were unmasked. Their lasting legacy was a remarkable book with the impressive Latin title *Vestiarium Scoticum* (Scottish Costume), which was a sensation when it appeared in 1842. It not only listed, but also illustrated no fewer than seventy-five tartans in gorgeous chromolithography. Their timing was impeccable, for that was the very year that Queen Victoria first visited Scotland and immediately fell in love with it.

Clans that never knew they had a tartan accepted the findings of the Sobieski Stuarts without question. More remarkably, no one appears to have questioned the inclusion of a number of prominent Lowland families, which, given the Lowland anathema to tartan in earlier centuries, was quite patently absurd. Ironically, many of the tartans invented by the Sobieski Stuarts and eagerly manufactured by Wilson's of Bannockburn now rank among the oldest, and therefore most authentic, tartans.

This established the precedent for creating new tartans that continues to this day and, in fact, has escalated out of all recognition in the past decade alone. Recognizing that this proliferation of tartans was in danger of getting out of control, the late Sir Thomas Innes of Learney, the Lord Lyon King of Arms, founded the Scottish Tartans Society in 1963. Today the society offers a wide range of services, from searching for the appropriate tartan for a surname, including its ancestry or circumstances, to helping members design a tartan of their very own. Arguably the most valuable work of the society consists of its register of tartans, a formidable undertaking in view of the new varieties that continue to appear, so far passing the 3,000 mark in numbers.

What started out as the distinctive check worn by the Highland clans has developed out of all recognition. The Sobieski Stuarts started the fashion for tartan among the Lowland families, but even they would be astonished at the Sikh and Singh tartans sported by some of Scotland's more recent settlers. Apart from Scots, who, in default of a claim to one of the clan or sept tartans, have commissioned their own family setts, there is also a vast range of trade tartans. Some of these trade tartans are also classified as corporate, although this term is mainly used to describe the tartans worn by just about everyone from airline stewardesses to bank staff and car salesmen.

There was a time when the pipe bands of regiments in India and other parts of the old British Empire wore the tartans of their commanding officers, but today pipe bands must have their own tartan. Not so many years ago, the Stockyard Kilties of Chicago were content to sport the bright Buchanan tartan, but doubtless they now have their own sett. The spectacular parade on the first anniversary of the September 11, 2001, terrorist attacks was memorable for the display of distinctive tartans worn by the pipe bands of the New York Police and Fire Departments, but these are only two out of the many hundreds of American tartans that range from the FBI to the Leathernecks (Marine Corps). There is even a Polaris tartan, which was actually worn by Americans serving at the submarine base on the Holy Loch.

Perhaps the greatest expansion in tartan is the extension of this fashion to Ireland, which is covered in some detail in the relevant section of this book. Significantly, the impetus for this has come not from Ireland itself (where plain green tartans are still preferred) but from people of Irish descent in Britain and overseas. Apart from the tartans representing the thirty-two counties and four historic provinces of Ireland, quite a number of Irish family tartans have now been created. Significantly, the impetus for these Irish tartans has come mainly from expatriate Irishmen or people of Irish descent living in North America, Australia, or New Zealand, countries where the Scottish tartan tradition has always been very strong.

This trend is moving to a logical conclusion, notably in the United States, where individual states are now registering distinctive setts. The latest of these, declared official by the state governor on July 23, 2002, is the California tartan, derived from the Muir tartan as a tribute to the contribution of the Scottish naturalist John Muir to the preservation of the scenery and wildlife of that state.

SCOTTISH TARTANS

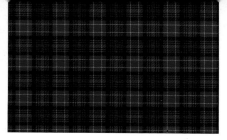

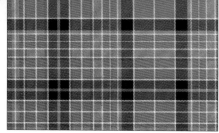

ABERCROMBIE

Badge: With Latin motto *Petit alta* (He
   desires the heights)
Gaelic: *Aber Crombaigh*

This family takes its name from the hamlet of
Abercrombie, about a mile north of St. Monans in
Fife. William de Abercromby was listed in the
Ragman Rolls (1296) as doing homage to Edward I.
The ancestral lands passed to a cadet branch,
the Abercrombies of Birkenbog, Banffshire,
in the seventeenth century. This family produced
a number of courtiers, notably Alexander
Abercromby, who was granted a baronet by
Charles I in 1636. His descendant, General Sir
Ralph Abercromby (1734–1801), was born near
Menstrie, Clackmannanshire, and was parliament
representative for that county (1774–80), but is best
remembered for his exploits in the West Indies and
Egypt during the Napoleonic Wars.

ABERDEEN

Badge: Three towers, with the French motto
   Bon Accord
Gaelic: *Abair-eadhain* (Between the mouths
   of the rivers Dee and Don)

The third-largest city in Scotland, Aberdeen was
the seat of a bishop from 1156 and the location of
two universities from the late sixteenth century. In
recent times it has become the oil capital of the
north. It is the proud possessor of one of the oldest
district tartans, registered by Wilson's of
Bannockburn in 1794, but apparently in existence
prior to that date. This is also one of the most
complex tartans, with no fewer than 446 threads to
the half-sett.

AGNEW

Badge: A perching bird with spread wings,
and the Latin motto *Consilio non impetu*
(By counsel, not force)
Gaelic: *Ui Gnimh*

Clan historians are divided on the origins of this name, some maintaining that it is derived from the Ulster bardic family of O'Gnew, which is believed to have migrated to Wigtownshire in the middle ages. Certainly by 1363, the Agnews of Lochnaw had become hereditary sheriffs of Galloway and from 1451 sheriffs of Wigtown, a title held by the clan chief to this day. Others, however, trace its origins to Agneaux in Normandy via Norman mercenaries who came from England to Scotland at the behest of King David I in the early twelfth century. The most famous (or notorious) of this name was Spiro Agnew (1918–96, vice president of the U.S. 1969–73).

ALEXANDER

Gaelic: *Alasdair*

This name is derived from the Greek, meaning "helper or defender of mankind." It was borne by several kings of Macedon (including Alexander the Great), three czars of Russia, and three kings of Scots in the twelfth and thirteenth centuries. It became one of the most popular Scottish forenames following the birth of Alexander I in 1107. As a surname it appears to have been associated with the Lords of the Isles, hence the Clan MacAlister, but in its English form, MacAlexander, it was associated with Stirlingshire. The Mac prefix was abandoned in the 1690s. From the Alexanders of Menstrie came the courtier-poet Sir William Alexander, first Earl of Stirling. More recent scions of the family were Field Marshal Earl Alexander of Tunis (1891–1969) and American baseball star Grover Alexander (1887–1950).

 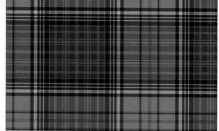

ALLISON

Gaelic: *Mac Alasdair* (Son of Alexander)

This name is borne by families, which are regarded as septs or branches of the MacDonalds and the MacAlisters, although there is considerable controversy over the origin of the name, and it has been plausibly argued that it is derived from Lowland Scots, meaning "son of Alice," the names Ellis, Ellice, Elson, and Ellison being variants of this. Interestingly, Allison as a girl's forename does not exist before about 1830. Although the clan now traces its origins to Alexander MacAlister of Loup, Lanarkshire, in the fourteenth century, Alissone appears in the Ragman Rolls (1296). Most famous of this name was Sir Archibald Allison, one of Glasgow's most prominent businessmen in the early nineteenth century.

ANDERSON

Badge: An oak tree, with the motto "Stand sure"
Gaelic: *Mac Ghille Aindreas* (Son of the servant or follower of St. Andrew)

This is the usual form of a name found all over Scotland, although its Highland counterpart is MacAndrew, a branch of the once-powerful Clan Chattan in Inverness-shire as far back as 1400. Famous clansmen include Dr. John Anderson, founder of the medical college, which is now Strathclyde University, and Arthur Anderson, the founder of the P&O shipping line.

ANGUS

Badge: A shield with four quarters bearing a lion passant gardant, a cinquefoil, a fess chequy surmounted by bend charged with three buckles, and a crowned heart with three mullets, derived from the arms of the Gillibride, Umfraville, Stewart, and Douglas Earls of Angus, with the motto *Lippen on Angus* (Trust in Angus)

Gaelic: *Aonghus* (Aeneas)

In the Middle Ages, Angus was one of the seven petty kingdoms of Scotland, ruled by a *mormaer* (governor). Its moment of fame came in 1320 when the nobility and clergy assembled at Arbroath and produced Scotland's declaration of independence. The family of this name claims descent from Oenghus, one of three Irish brothers who established the kingdom of Dalriada in Argyll, although this seems more properly the origins of the clan MacInnes. Angus was (and still is) a very common forename and probably the widespread use of it as a surname originates from that. The tartan is both a family and a district tartan; the former county of Angus (also known as Forfarshire) later became a district of the Tayside region.

ARBUTHNOTT

Badge: A peacock's head, with the Latin motto *Laus Deo* (Praise God)

Gaelic: *Aber Bothenoth* (Mouth of the stream below the noble house)

Hugh of Swinton acquired the lands of Arbuthnott, Kincardineshire, through marriage to the daughter of Osbert Olifard the Crusader at the beginning of the thirteenth century. By 1355 Philip de Arbuthnott was using the title "of that ilk" and a century later his descendant, Sir Robert, was declared first Viscount Arbuthnott and Baron Inverbervie. The most famous member of this family was Dr. John Arbuthnott (1667–1735), political satirist and physician to the royal family.

ARGYLL

Badge: A lymphad (galley) surmounted by a fess chequy, above which is a gyronny and a wing holding a crowned sword, with the Gaelic motto *Seas ar coir* (Maintain our right)

Gaelic: *Earraghaidheal* (The land of the far or westerly Gaels)

Although this tartan is worn by people with Argyll or Argyle as a surname, it is more specifically a district tartan, created by Wilson's of Bannockburn in 1819 and clearly derived from the sett of the Campbells, the dominant clan of the former county. It is very similar to that of Campbell of Cawdor and was formerly worn by the Ninety-first Foot (Argyllshire Highlanders). Argyll was settled by the Scotti from Ireland in the fifth century and became their kingdom of Dalriada before they expanded eastward and northward to wrest the country from the Picts.

ARMSTRONG

Badge: An arm raised in salute, with the
   Latin motto *Invictus maneo* (I remain
   unconquered)
Gaelic: *Mac Ghille Laidir* (Son of the strong
   servant)

One of the most powerful of the Border clans, the
Armstrongs trace their origin to Fairbairn, a strong
man who had the honor of carrying the king's
armor and who, according to tradition, was
rewarded for his services with lands in Liddesdale.
The ballad of Johnny Armstrong recalls the hanging
of a famous Border raider and thirty of his
henchmen at Carlingrigg in the reign of James V.
The most famous member of the clan in more
recent times is Neil Armstrong, who has the honor
of being the first man on the Moon.

ARRAN

Badge: A fess between three cross-crosslets
   with the Latin motto *In hoc signo vinces*
   (In this sign conquer)
Gaelic: *Aran* (Bread)

This island in the Firth of Clyde has long been
extremely popular with vacationers from Glasgow
and the southwest of Scotland, but increasingly
also with overseas tourists. Easily accessible from
the Clyde ports, it combines the scenery of the
Lowlands and Highlands, dominated by its central
mountains. Gaelic was still spoken in Arran in the
nineteenth century and most of its place-names
are of Gaelic origin. It has historical connections
with Robert the Bruce and the powerful Hamilton
family with their stronghold at Brodick Castle.
Arran's distinctive tartans were created by
McNaughtons of Pitlochry in 1982, and a second
sett has a blue ground.

ATHOLL

Badge: A demi-savage holding a dagger and
   a key, with the French motto *Tout prest*
   (Always ready)
Gaelic: *Athall*

The ancient earldom of Atholl or Athole was
conferred on Sir John Stewart in 1457, but passed
to John Murray, Earl of Tullibardine, in 1629
following his marriage to the fifth earl's daughter
and heiress. Through marriage to a Stanley heiress,
the first Duke of Atholl also became Lord of Man,
but sold his rights to that island in 1765. The Atholl
tartan is one of the oldest of the district tartans, in
existence since the early seventeenth century, and
used as a military tartan from the 1740s. Its colors
and pattern have affinities with the clan tartans of
the district, both Murray of Atholl and Robertson.

AULD REEKIE

This is a fine example of a modern trade tartan, in
this particular instance designed in 1997 for
Burkcraft Limited and applied to a wide range of
tartan goods, from traveling rugs to ties and
scarves as well as kilts and plaids. The name is
Lowland Scots for "Old Smokey" and is the
popular nickname for Edinburgh, which, in an age
before smokeless fuels, had a bad reputation
(especially on the north shore of the Firth of Forth,
where the people of Fife joked that one could tell
the time of day by the amount of smoke rising from
the city's chimneys.) The term was popularized by
Robert Fergusson (1750–74) in his poem of the
same name, an affectionate ode to his hometown
published shortly before his untimely death.

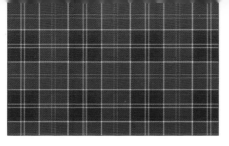 

AYRSHIRE

Badge: A three-towered castle, a red
  chevron, a shakefork, and a fess chequy
  (the arms of Ayr, Carrick, Cunningham,
  and Kyle) with the Scots motto *God
  schaw the richt* (God shows the right)

This ancient county on the east shore of the Firth of
Clyde became part of the Strathclyde region in the
1970s and its districts named after the ancient
baileries of Cunningham, Kyle, and Carrick, but in
the restructuring of the 1990s the old county name
was restored. While Ayrshire was in limbo, Dr. Philip
Smith designed this district tartan at the behest of
the Boyd and Cunningham clan societies. Its colors
represent different characteristics of the area
during the course of a day: yellow for the rising sun,
green for the hills and farmlands, brown for the
coast, blue for the sea, and red for the setting sun.

BAILLIE

Badge: A boar's head, with the Latin motto
  Quid clarius astris? (What is brighter than
  the stars?)

This surname has various spellings and is from the
Scots form of "bailiff," a word derived from the Latin
bajulus (a porter) via Norman-French *baillier* (to
have in charge). Baillie originally meant "a royal
officer," but is now used in local government as the
equivalent of the English alderman, a superior rank
of councillor. The Baillies of Lamington trace their
origins back to Sir William Baillie, son of William de
Balliol. He changed his name to distance himself
from the disastrous reign of John Balliol, King of
Scots in 1292–96. The tartan was created by
Wilson's of Bannockburn in 1794 for the Baillie
Fencibles, one of the militia regiments raised at the
outbreak of the French Revolutionary Wars.
Famous names include photographer David Bailey.

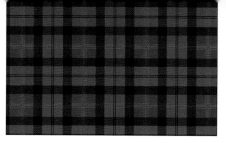
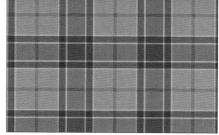

BAIRD

Badge: An eagle's head, with the Latin motto
  Dominus fecit (The Lord made it)
Gaelic: *Mac a Bhaird* (Son of the bard or
  poet)

Early in the thirteenth century a Baird was given the
estates of Kype in Lanarkshire by William the Lion
for saving the king's life from a wild boar, while
Robert Baird was granted the barony of
Cambusnethan by King Robert Bruce and
descendants acquired lands in Banffshire and
Aberdeenshire. Famous Bairds include General Sir
David (1757–1829), hero of wars in India and the
Peninsular campaign, and John Logie Baird, the
inventor of television.

BALFOUR

Badge: A chevron bearing three otters' heads,
  with three mullets in the field and the Latin
  motto *Virtus ad aethera tendet* (Let valor
  reach out into space)

Balfour was the name of a seat near Kirriemuir in
Fife, now remembered solely by the ruins of Balfour
Castle. The village of Balfour in Orkney is apparently
unconnected. John de Balfure is named in an assize
summons of 1304 and numerous references to this
family appear in Fife after that time. Famous names
include George Balfour (1872–1941), the electrical
engineer and pioneering contractor; Francis Balfour
(1851–82), the pioneer of embryology; and his elder
brother Arthur (1848–1930), the philosopher-turned-
statesman, best remembered for the Balfour
Declaration (1917). For his time spent as Prime
Minister and Leader of the House of Commons, he
was made Earl Balfour of Whittinghame.

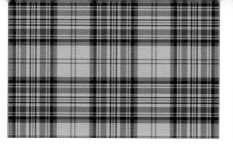 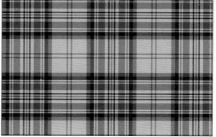

BALMORAL

This name, originally Bouchmorale, was a seat of the Gordon family for centuries, but in 1662 it was sold to the Farquharsons of Inverey. In turn they sold it to the Earl of Fife in 1798 and he let it to Sir Robert Gordon. The tenancy became vacant on his death in 1848 and it was then taken up by Prince Albert, the Prince Consort, who purchased it in 1852 for £31,500. It has since been the personal holiday home of the Royal Family. It is believed that the various Balmoral tartans were designed by Prince Albert himself, initially as wall coverings but later adapted to kilts and other articles of dress. Of the five tartans, the one illustrated is the dress tartan, intended for evening wear. It is now often used by Scots (or indeed any subject of the Queen) in default of a clan, district, or personal tartan.

BALMORAL GILLIES

Another of the setts associated with the royal residence on Deeside is this tartan, which derives its name from the fact that it was originally intended to be worn by the gillies (gamekeepers) on the royal estate. The word is derived from the Gaelic *gille*, meaning "servant." In a sense, the provision of a special tartan for the royal Highland servants is akin to the livery provided for servants of great families elsewhere. It carries on the tradition of the nineteenth century, in which tartans in muted colors, known as estate checks, were worn by the outdoor servants who accompanied shooting, hunting, and fishing parties. This particular tartan is believed to date from the interwar period. A sample is preserved in the MacGregor-Hastie Collection in the Mitchell Library, Glasgow, formed between 1930 and 1950. A similar tartan, without the red stripes, is known as the Balmoral Green Lines and presumably dates from the same period.

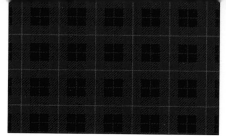

BARCLAY

BAXTER

Badge: A hand holding a dagger, with the Latin motto *Aut agere aut mori* (Action or death)

Motto: *Vincit veritas* (Truth prevails)

The progenitor of this clan was a Norman named Walter de Berkeley, one of the officials recruited by King David I to reorganize the administration of the kingdom, but the present form of the name first appears in the late fourteenth century. The name is prevalent in Kincardineshire, Aberdeenshire, and Fife. Clansmen include James Barclay of Urie, who became a prominent London banker. From the Barclays of Towie in Aberdeenshire came Field Marshal Prince Michael Barclay de Tolly, ennobled by the czar for helping to rid Russia of Napoleon.

This name comes from a Lowland Scots word meaning "female baker." Consequently it is a trade name, found all over Scotland, although it seems to have been more common in Fife, Angus, and Kincardine, represented by several landed families, such as the Baxters of Earlshall near St. Andrews. Prominent people of this name include the celebrated theologian Richard Baxter (1615–91), who was both chaplain to Cromwell and Charles II; David Baxter (1793–1872), founder of modern Dundee; John Baxter (1781–1856), inventor of the ink-roller and publisher of the earliest rules of cricket; the New Zealand playwright John Baxter; and the Fochabers firm of Baxter's Soups, whose products are enjoyed worldwide.

BERWICK-UPON-TWEED

Badge: A bear tethered to a wych-elm, with
   the Latin motto *Victoria gloria merces*
   (Glory is the reward of valor)

In the Middle Ages, Berwick-upon-Tweed was one of the four royal burghs of Scotland, second in size only to Edinburgh. It owed its importance to the fact that it was strategically placed at the mouth of the Tweed, guarding the eastern end of the border between Scotland and England.

In 1296, it was sacked by Edward I and its inhabitants slaughtered, the worst atrocity in Anglo-Scottish history. Although Edward rebuilt the town and granted a charter in 1302, it was continually fought over and changed hands many times until 1482, when it became irrevocably English. It became a free town in 1551 and a separate county in 1836. On account of its special status, it was named separately in acts of parliament and proclamations. Technically, Berwick is still at war with Russia, as it was named in the declaration at the beginning of the Crimean War, but not named in the peace treaty. The district tartan was commissioned in 1982 to celebrate the quincentenary of Berwick as an English town, which seems contradictory to say the least; but both geographically and ethnically, the Scottish character of Berwick remains strong. Significantly, the arms of Berwick-upon-Tweed were granted in 1958 by the Lord Lyon in Edinburgh, rather than the Garter King of Arms in London, under the "ancient user" privilege.

BETHUNE

BLACK WATCH

Badge: A demi-otter, with the motto
  Debonnaire
Gaelic: *Beutan*

Badge: St. Andrew and his saltire cross
  flanked by thistles, with the Latin motto
  Nemo me impune lacessit (No one
  touches me with impunity)
Gaelic: *Am Freiceadan Dubh*

Bethune in Northern France is the origin of this family, which was among those that came to England during the Norman Conquest and then migrated to Scotland in the reign of David I. By 1165, Robert de Bethunia is recorded as the witness to a charter. A century later, however, the names Bethune and Beaton were often interchangeable, although the Beatons are alleged to have been a branch of the MacBeth family. Both Beatons and Bethunes produced generations of physicians and surgeons, notably the Beatons of Mull, who were hereditary doctors to the MacLeans of Duart. The most famous was Norman Bethune (1899–1939), the Canadian surgeon who became a Chinese national hero during the Japanese war of 1937–39.

Blackmail was originally the crime of cattle rustling in the Highlands and it was in a bid to stamp out this black trade that a body of troops was raised in 1739 as a watch (police), hence the name of the Black Watch, by which the Royal Highlanders are popularly known. The tartan selected for this regiment was of very somber colors: dark green and blue. This tartan may have derived from the Campbell (because many of the regiment's officers belonged to that clan), but it is more probable that the Campbell tartan was derived from the Black Watch. It is regarded as one of the oldest tartans and is also known as the Government tartan.

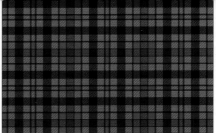

BLAIR

Badge: A bird with spreading wings, with the
   Latin motto *Virtute tutus* (Protected by valor)
Gaelic: *Blàr* (A field)

As a prefix, this word appears in many place-names, from Blairbeth to Blairtummel and Blairs, but the secondary meaning of the Gaelic word is "battlefield," which points to the military origins of the clan. The name appears from the early thirteenth century as Blare or Blair, mainly in Renfrewshire and the Cunningham district of Ayrshire. John Blair was chaplain to William Wallace and wrote an account of his exploits. The Blairs of Blair and Dunskey were prominent in business and politics in the eighteenth century. The most famous persons of this name include the preacher-poet Robert Blair (1699–1746), Eric Blair (the novelist George Orwell), and Tony Blair, the British Prime Minister.

BORTHWICK

Badge: A Moor's head, with the Latin motto
   Qui conducit (Who serves)

This powerful Border clan claims to trace its roots back to Roman times, although the first recorded members were in the retinue of the Anglo-Saxon Princess Margaret, who married Malcolm Canmore in 1069, and were given the lands of Borthwick in Roxburghshire. Sir William Borthwick was constable of Edinburgh Castle in the early fifteenth century and his son William raised to the peerage in 1450. He built Borthwick Castle, where Mary, Queen of Scots, honeymooning with Bothwell in 1567, was besieged by the rebel lords and escaped disguised as a boy. The castle still survives intact.

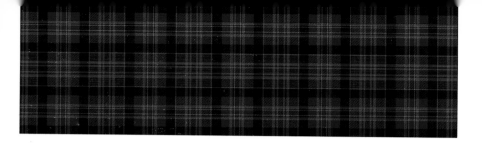

BOWIE

Gaelic: *Buidhe* (Fair or yellow-haired) or *Mac Ghille Buidhe* (Son of the fair-haired servant)

From the Gaelic names come the surnames Buie, Bowie, or MacIlbowie, variants of which have been recorded in Mull and the mainland of Argyll, where they were followers of the MacDonald Lords of the Isles. The surname also occurs in Inverness-shire and relates to a separate family that is regarded as a sept of Clan Grant. John Bowey was captain of Dumbarton Castle and held it against James IV on behalf of the rebels who had conspired against James III, though he was subsequently pardoned. Jerome Bowie was master of the royal wine cellars in 1585–89 and this form of the name was common in Stirling and Dunblane from the seventeenth century. The name will always be associated with the sheath-knife invented by Jim Bowie (1796–1836), born in Kentucky of Scottish descent and killed in the defense of the Alamo.

BOYD

Badge: A hand raised to swear an oath, with
the Latin motto *Confide* (Be trustful)
Gaelic: *Bóid* (Oath or vow) or *Buidhe*
(Yellow-haired)

The origins of this surname may have come from its
first recorded holder, Sir Robert Boyd, hero of the
battle of Largs (1263), who was yellow-haired.
However, the Gaelic word for the island of Bute, the
clan badge, and motto point to its derivation as the
word for "oath." Whatever the truth, the family is
actually of Breton origin, coming from Dol, where
they were hereditary stewards. Sir Robert's
grandson fought with distinction at Bannockburn
(1314) and received the barony of Kilmarnock as a
result. A later Robert was raised to the peerage in
the 1460s. William Boyd was made Earl of
Kilmarnock in 1661. Prominent members include
the biologist and Nobel Prize–winner Lord Boyd Orr.

BRAVEHEART

This is a name of very recent origin that has been
applied retrospectively to Scotland's greatest
patriot, William Wallace, and will be associated with
him forevermore. The first of the three tartans
bearing this name had nothing to do with Wallace
or the movie, but was produced in 1993 by Michael
King for a Scottish martial arts champion named
Watt who took part in the Japanese international
competition under the name of Braveheart Warrior.
The name Braveheart was adopted by Mel Gibson
for his epic movie two years later, and it sprang to
international prominence. However, there is no
evidence that the term was ever applied to Wallace
prior to that time, far less to the hero himself in his
lifetime. Although tartan features prominently (and
anachronistically) in the film, it bears no
resemblance to an identifiable sett. Michael King
subsequently designed dress and hunting
Braveheart Warrior tartans.

BRODIE

Badge: A hand holding three arrows, with
the motto "Unite"
Gaelic: *Brothaigh*

This clan takes its name from a district in Moray.
Michael, Thane of Brodie, was ennobled by King
Robert Bruce in 1312, although Brodie Castle has
been the family seat since the eleventh century.
The clan chief has the distinction of being the head
of one of the oldest untitled families, and is known
as Brodie of Brodie or just Brodie without a prefix.
Alexander Brodie of Brodie (1617–79) negotiated
the restoration of Charles II (1660), while his
grandson of the same name was Lord Lyon King of
Arms (1727–54). The most notorious Brodie was
the Edinburgh Deacon, allegedly the model for
Stevenson's *The Strange Case of Dr. Jekyll and
Mr. Hyde*.

BROWN

Badge: A lion rampant, with the Latin motto
Famae studiosus honestae (Earnestly
seeking after honest fame)

One of the most common surnames in Scotland, it
is derived from the French *brun* (brown-haired) and
probably came into English usage after the Norman
Conquest. A family named Le Brun was granted
lands in Cumbria by William the Conqueror and
Patrick and Richard Brown (or Broun) are recorded
as witnesses to a document in the reign of William
the Lyon (1194–1214). The Brouns of Colstoun in
East Lothian have held their lands since the early
fourteenth century, and from their motto and
emblem allude to their kinship with the royal house
of France. Famous bearers of the surname include
the militant abolitionist John Brown (1800–59) and
his namesake, Queen Victoria's faithful servant
(1826–83).

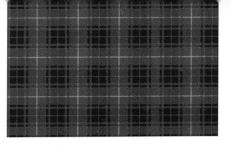

BRUCE

BRUCE OF KINNAIRD

Badge: A lion statant, tail extended, with the
   Latin motto *Fuimus* (We have been)
Gaelic: *Brus*

Although the name Brus was common among the
Vikings of the northern and western isles, this clan
derives from the powerful family that came to
Scotland, via Normandy and England, in the reign
of David I, and had extensive estates in Essex
and Yorkshire as well as Annandale and Carrick.
Robert Bruce, Lord of Annandale and Earl of
Carrick (1274–1329), renewed the struggle for
independence in 1306 and decisively defeated the
English at Bannockburn. Descendants include the
Earls of Elgin, Sir Michael Bruce (author of *Tramp
Royal*), and his brother, the actor Nigel Bruce, best
remembered for his part as Dr. Watson to Basil
Rathbone's Sherlock Holmes.

A prolific clan such as Bruce has many branches
and several of these have their own tartan. The
most distinctive of these is worn by the Bruces of
Kinnaird, who trace their origins all the way back to
the royal line via the Bruces of Airth and
Clackmannan. During his tour of Stirling and
Clackmannanshire in 1787, Robert Burns met Mrs.
Bruce of Clackmannan, who knighted him with the
sword allegedly carried by her royal ancestor at
Bannockburn. The most celebrated member of this
family was James Bruce (1730–94), known as
"Abyssinian" Bruce for his exploration of the Nile
(1770) and the discovery of the headwaters of the
Blue Nile.

BUCCLEUCH

Badge: A stag trippant proper, with the Latin motto *Amo* (I love)

This name originates from a place on the Rankle Burn eleven miles west of Hawick in the Scottish Borders and from it the noble family of Montagu-Douglas-Scott derive their ducal title. Of the two Buccleuch tartans, the first was designed as a regimental tartan during the Napoleonic Wars and is worn by pipers of the King's Own Scottish Borderers. The clan tartan shown here was devised by Wilson's of Bannockburn in the 1830s and was originally designated as a "fancy pattern" (for general use and not for a particular clan). Its name was a tribute to Sir Walter Scott, who had done so much to popularize tartan. Although the great novelist belonged to another branch of the Scotts, the tartan was appropriated by Sir Richard Scott and associated with the Buccleuch family ever since.

BUCHAN

Badge: Three lions' heads, with the Latin motto *Non inferiora secutus* (Not having followed inferior things)

The northeasterly district of Aberdeenshire was governed in Celtic times by mormaers, from whom the later Earls of Buchan were derived. In the Middle Ages this earldom was in the hands of the powerful Comyn family and a close association with the Comyns and Cummings continues to this day. Andrew de Buchan was Bishop of Caithness in the early fourteenth century and the Buchans of Auchmacoy received their lands in 1318. Prominent members include the meteorologist Alexander Buchan (1829–1907), who formulated the theory of climate cycles known as Buchan spells, and the writer and statesman John Buchan (1875–1940). The Buchanites religious sect was founded by Elspeth Buchan (1738–91).

BUCHANAN

Badge: A right hand holding a ducal coronet,
   with the Latin motto *Audaces juvo*
   (I prefer the brave)
Gaelic: *Canonach*

Auslan or Absalon O Kyan, a prince of Ulster, settled in Argyll around 1016 and for his services against the Danes at Clontarf, he was granted the lands of Both-chanain (canon's seat) east of Loch Lomond. The estate remained in the family's hands until 1682, but other branches held extensive lands in Stirlingshire and Dunbartonshire. Famous clansmen include George Buchanan (1506–82), the foremost Latin scholar of his day and tutor to Mary, Queen of Scots; Andrew Buchanan, the tobacco lord, who laid out Glasgow's most popular shopping street; and James Buchanan, fifteenth president of the United States.

BURNETT

Badge: A cubit arm pruning a vine, with the
   Latin motto *Virescit vulnere virtus* (Courage
   gains strength from a wound)

This important Aberdeenshire family traces its ancestry back to the Anglo-Saxon Beornhard, which by the middle of the thirteenth century had become Burnard. In 1324, Alexander Burnard was granted the Forest of Drum and the barony of Tulliboyl in Aberdeenshire by Robert the Bruce, betokened by an ivory hunting horn encrusted with jewels, a prized heirloom of the Burnetts of Leys now on show in Crathes Castle, the family seat that was gifted to the National Trust for Scotland. Thomas Burnet of Leys was granted a baronet in 1626 and his son Sir Alexander added the second "t" to the surname. Famous members of this family include the historian Gilbert Burnet, and the writers Frances Burnett and Ivy Compton-Burnett.

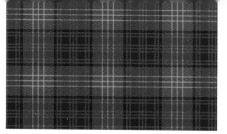

BURNS

Badge: A tree over a shepherd's crook and
    stock-horn, with the motto "Better a wee
    bush than nae bield (shelter)"

The myth that the Burns family were renegade
Campbells of Burnhouse in Argyll persists despite
the fact that it was proven false at least 150 years
ago. Burns (Burnes or Burness) is a common name
all over Scotland and derives from the word for
"stream" or from the Norse name Bjorn. The most
famous branch of the family was holding land in the
Glenbervie district of Kincardineshire at least from
1329. William Burnes (1721–84), the youngest of
three brothers from Clochnahill, migrated to
Ayrshire and became the father of Robert Burns,
Scotland's national bard. Another brother moved to
Montrose, and his grandson was Sir Alexander
Burns, whose murder triggered off the first Afghan
War in 1839.

BURNS, ROBERT

This check, although impeccably Scottish in its
intentions and uses, is unusual if not unique in that
it was devised by a Belgian aristocrat, Baron
Georges Marchand, to mark the bicentenary of the
birth of Scotland's national bard in 1959. He
presented it to the Burns Federation, the
worldwide organization of Burns clubs and
Scottish societies, which has its headquarters in
Kilmarnock, where Burns's poems were first
published in book form in 1786. Marchand took as
the basis of this tartan the simple black-and-white
check that was commonly worn in the Lowlands in
the poet's lifetime, but added subtle shades of
green and brown to represent the Ayrshire
countryside. Although used primarily by the Burns
Federation to this day, the Robert Burns check is
also extensively used in the packaging of Burns
souvenirs officially approved by the Federation.

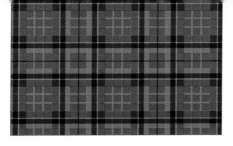

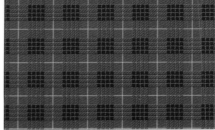

CALEDONIA

CAMERON

Wilson's of Bannockburn created this, the first of the universal tartans, in 1819 in order to provide all Scots who did not possess a clan tartan the opportunity to wear the kilt. Its name comes from the Caledonii, the martial tribe that the Romans held at bay by erecting Hadrian's Wall. After many centuries in oblivion, the name was revived in the eighteenth century by poets and within fifty years Caledonia had become widely established as an alternative name for Scotland, reflected in the Caledonian Bank (1838), Caledonian Railway (1845), and Caledonian Canal (1847), and in many other institutions of more recent times, as well as the Pacific Island group known as New Caledonia (which, incidentally, now has its own tartan).

Badge: An arm in armor, the hand holding a sword, with the Latin motto *Pro rege et patria* (For king and country)

Gaelic: *Camshron* (Crooked nose)

One of the oldest clans of Scotland, the Camerons have occupied lands in Lochaber since the late thirteenth century, if not earlier. Within this large clan there are several important branches, each with its own badge and tartan, noted separately, although they spring from a common source. By the fifteenth century the most powerful branches of the clan were the MacMartins of Letterfinlay, the MacGillonies of Strone, and the MacSorleys of Glen Nevis. The clan was allied to the Lord of the Isles and fought under his banner at Harlaw in 1411, but later they broke away.

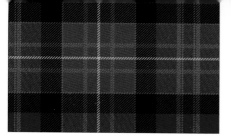

CAMERON OF ERRACHT

Badge: St. Andrew holding his saltire cross
Gaelic: *Camshron* (Crooked nose)

This important branch of the Clan Cameron is derived from Ewen, son of Ewen the clan chief and his second wife, Marjory MacKintosh, early in the sixteenth century. Donald Cameron of Erracht was a staunch supporter of Prince Charles but fled into exile after Culloden. His son Allan served in the American Revolutionary War and in 1793 raised the Cameron Highlanders for service in the French Revolutionary War. As the 79th Foot, the regiment has a long and honorable history in the British Army.

CAMERON OF LOCHEIL

Badge: Five arrows bound together, with the
Gaelic motto *Aonaibh ri cheile* (Joined to one another)
Gaelic: *Camshron* (Crooked nose)

This major branch of the Camerons traces its descent from the MacGillonies of Strone, later strengthened by intermarriage with the MacMartins of Letterfinlay. By 1528 Cameron of Locheil had emerged as Captain of Clan Cameron and was named as such in a charter from James V. Achnacarry, the clan seat since the seventeenth century, was destroyed by the Duke of Cumberland in 1746 but rebuilt in 1802–37. During World War II it was an important commando training base.

CAMPBELL

Badge: A boar's head, with the Latin motto
   Ne obliviscaris (Do not forget)
Gaelic: *Caimbeul* (Wry-mouth)

This powerful clan traces its origins to Malcolm MacDiarmid, who married a Norman heiress named Beauchamp early in the eleventh century. Their son, Archibald, came to England with the Conqueror in 1066 and was the progenitor of the Beauchamp and Beecham families. The name, meaning "beautiful field," was rendered in medieval Latin as Campobello, and from this came Kemble and Campbell. Colin Campbell of Lochow, knighted in 1280, founded the Argyll clan, whose spectacular rise is charted in the fortunes of its chiefs, who were raised to the peerage (1445), given an earldom (1457), a marquessate (1641), and finally a dukedom (1690).

CAMPBELL OF ARGYLL

Badge: A boar's head with the Latin motto
   Ne obliviscaris (Do not forget)
Gaelic: *Caimbeul* (Wry-mouth)

The senior branch of Clan Campbell includes the name of the county, which was their traditional power base. The chief of the clan is known in Gaelic as *Mac Cailein Mór* (the son of Great Colin), a reference to Colin of Lochow, the progenitor of the clan. For two centuries the Campbells fought the MacDougalls of Lorne for the ascendancy in Argyll, but after 1445 their power was assured and unassailed. In 1618 the Earl of Argyll took over Lochhead on the southeast coast of Kintyre and expanded it considerably. Its name was officially changed to Campbeltown in 1667 and it was raised to the status of a royal burgh in 1700. The Campbell of Argyll tartan is similar to the main Campbell tartan but with opposing white and yellow stripes.

CAMPBELL OF BREADALBANE

CAMPBELL OF CAWDOR

Badge: A boar's head, with the motto
"Follow me"
Gaelic: *Caimbeul* (Wry-mouth)

Badge: A crowned swan, with the motto
"Be mindful"
Gaelic: *Caimbeul* (Wry-mouth)

This branch of the clan originated with Sir Colin Campbell of Lochow, who acquired lands in Lorne by marriage, built Kilchurn Castle, and distinguished himself in the Crusades. His descendants extended their lands in Argyll and Perthshire by judicious marriages. Sir John Campbell was named Earl of Breadalbane in 1681 and this title became a marquessate of the United Kingdom peerage in 1831, but the death of John, the fifth earl, in 1862 brought this title to an end. It was conferred on Gavin, the seventh earl, in 1885, but he died without issue in 1922 and the title has been defunct ever since.

In 1510, Sir John Campbell, third son of the second Earl of Argyll, married Muriel, daughter of Sir John Calder of Calder in Nairnshire, through whom the ancient title of Thane of Cawdor (once borne by MacBeth) passed to their grandson John Campbell. Marriage with a Pryce heiress in the eighteenth century brought extensive estates in Pembrokeshire. John Campbell, named Baron Cawdor in 1796, is remembered for defeating the French at Fishguard in 1797, the last foreign invasion of British soil. His son was named Earl of Cawdor in 1827, taking the courtesy title of Viscount Emlyn from his Welsh estates.

CARLISLE

Badge: A lion statant gardant, with the
  Latin motto *Volo non valeo* (I am willing
  if not able)

At first glance it might be supposed that this was a district tartan for the border town, which on account of its position has close affinities with Annandale and Galloway. In fact, it is a good example of a personal tartan, designed as recently as 1987 at the behest of Christopher Carlisle Justus of North Carolina. The sett of pale blue and yellow bands with contrasting stripes of red and dark blue are derived from his own arms. Carlisle (and its older variant, Carlyle) is a common surname in Dumfriesshire. The most famous bearer of the name was, of course, the great historian and essayist, Thomas Carlyle (1795–1881). Although latterly known as the Sage of Chelsea, he was born at Ecclefechan and spent the first forty years of his life in his home county. In more recent years, prominent members of the family have included Wilson Carlile, founder of the Church Army, and the actor Robert Carlisle.

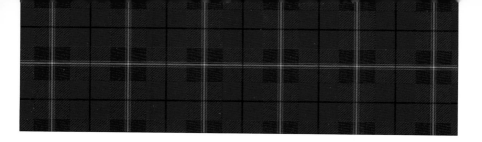

CARMICHAEL

Badge: A hand grasping a broken lance, with the French motto *Toujour prest* (Always ready)

Gaelic: *Caer Micheil* (Michael's fort)

This prominent family derives its name from the barony of this name in the Upper Ward of Lanarkshire. A Robert de Caramicely features in a document of 1226, although the barony was not granted to Sir John Carmichael until about 1380. Mary Carmichael was one of the Four Maries, ladies-in-waiting to Mary, Queen of Scots. Sir James Carmichael (1579–1672) was raised to the peerage in 1647 while his grandson John, first Earl of Hyndford (1701), was Scotland's last Lord Chancellor before the Union of 1707. The unusual motif in the clan badge alludes to an incident at the Battle of Beauge in 1421 during the Hundred Years' War. Sir John de Carmichael fought in the Scots contingent on the French side against the English and broke his lance in the act of unseating the Duke of Clarence. Other famous clan members include the jazz pianist and composer Hoagy Carmichael and the civil rights activist Stokely Carmichael.

CARNEGIE

Badge: A winged thunderbolt, with the motto
"Dred God"

The Norman knight Jocelyn de Ballinhard received
the lands of Carnegie in Angus from William the
Lyon in 1203 and possession was confirmed by
David II in 1358. The main line died out in 1563 but
the title and lands passed eventually to Sir David
Carnegie of Kinnaird (1575–1628), raised to the
peerage in 1616 and named Earl of Southesk in
1633. His younger brother, John of Ethie
(1579–1667), became Earl of Northesk in 1666.
Both earldoms are still extant, although the most
famous member of the clan was Andrew Carnegie
(1835–1919), the industrialist and philanthropist.
Having made a vast fortune in America, Carnegie
spent his later years at Skibo Castle in Sutherland.
Carnegie Hall (New York) and Carnegie libraries all
over the world are his permanent memorial.

CELTIC F. C.

Brother Walfrid, a Catholic priest from Dumfries,
ministered to the poor in Glasgow and in the course
of this mission formed a soccer team in 1888. Its
name alludes to the Celtic traditions of Christianity
that go all the way back to St. Columba in the sixth
century, a reminder of the Irish origins of the Scots
as well as a tribute to the many Irish immigrants.
Predominantly (though not exclusively) Catholic in
the religious persuasion of its players, Celtics and
their traditional rivals, Rangers, are known as the
Old Firm, towering over all the other soccer teams
in Scotland in their consistently premier position.
This tartan, designed for the team's supporters, is
based on the club's uniform, which consists of
green and white horizontal stripes. It was produced
by Tartan Sportswear and launched by team
captain Billy McNeil on St. Andrew's Day in 1989. It
has since been replaced by another sett, after
Tartan Sportswear went into liquidation.

CHILDERS

This is an ancient Scottish Lowland family that has left its mark on the history of Britain, Australia, and Ireland over the last two centuries. While some of its members rose to prominence in the Church, others entered the colonial service. They include Robert Caesar Childers (1838–76), who was a civil servant in Ceylon (now Sri Lanka) and became one of the foremost Asian scholars of his day. His son, Robert Erskine Childers (1870–1922), was the novelist who wrote the classic *Riddle of the Sands* and was successively House of Commons Clerk, trooper in the Boer War, and air ace in World War I. He joined the Irish Republican Army and was executed by a Nationalist firing squad. His son, Erskine Hamilton Childers (1905–74), was latterly President of Ireland. Hugh C. E. Childers (1827–96) had a distinguished career in Australia before entering British politics in 1860 and held many cabinet posts in successive Liberal governments. As Secretary for War (1880–82) he reorganized the British Army and devised this tartan in the hope that it would be adopted by all the Highland regiments. They successfully opposed this and today the Childers tartan is confined to the Gurkha Rifles pipe band.

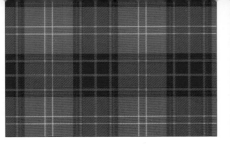

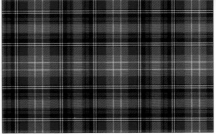

CHISHOLM

Badge: A boar's head impaled on a
    handheld dagger, with the Latin motto
    Feros ferio (I strike the fierce)
Gaelic: *Siosal*

Although this clan is firmly associated with the
Highlands, with lands in Erchless and Strathglass,
it is actually of Norman origin and derives its name
from Chesilholm (gravel holm) in Roxburghshire.
The family held lands in Berwickshire, but the
move north came in the late twelfth century when
a Chisholm became Thane of Caithness. Sir
Robert Chisholm became constable of Urqhuart
Castle on Loch Ness in 1359 and his son
Alexander married the heiress of Erchless, which
has been the clan seat ever since. The Chisholms
were ardent Jacobites, successive chiefs
distinguishing themselves at Sheriffmuir (1715)
and Culloden (1746).

CHRISTIE

This name probably arose as a diminutive form of
Christopher or Christian and associated with it is
the patronymic form Christison. Both Christie and
Christison are common surnames in Fife and
Stirlingshire, although also widespread in other
parts of Scotland and traditionally regarded as a
sept of the Farquharsons. The earliest reference to
the name pertains to John Chrysty, mentioned as a
burgess of Newburgh in 1457, and over the
ensuing century there are numerous other variants
of the name in documents and charters, mainly in
Fife. Famous persons of this name include William
Christie (1748–1823), the first Unitarian minister in
Scotland; James Christie (1730–1803), founder of
the auction house; the actress Julie Christie; and
the athlete Linford Christie, as well as the notorious
serial killer John Christie (1898–1953).

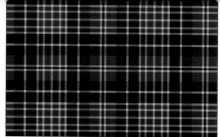

CLAN CHATTAN

Badge: A cat salient, with the motto "Touch
   not the cat bot (without) a glove"
Gaelic: *Clann Gillechatan*

This is a superclan or confederation of clans, the
individual members of which have as their emblem
a cat in various guises. The Clan of the Cats was a
close alliance in the north of Scotland as far back
as the late twelfth century, and eventually
comprised the Davidsons, Farquharsons,
Mackintoshes, MacPhersons, MacGillivrays, and
MacBeans. The first chief was the eleventh-
century Gillechattan Mor, whose descendant Eva
married Angus, sixth Laird of MacIntosh, Captain of
Clan Chattan. His claim to the chiefship was
contested by the chief of the clan MacPherson and
this led to a long-running feud between the
Mackintoshes and the MacPhersons, which
rumbles on to this day.

CLARK

Badge: The head of a unicorn, with the Latin
   motto *Perseverantia cum perceptione*
   (Perseverance with perception)
Gaelic: *Cléireach* (Clerk or writer)

This occupational surname derives from the Latin
clericus (clerk or cleric), denoting a monk or scribe.
It later referred to a scholar in general and has various
forms such as Clerk, Clerke, Clark, or Clarke. Clan
Clerich, for example, was one of the original
seventeen branches of Clan Chattan. The family of
Clerke of Ulva is descended from Francis William
Clark, who changed his name when he acquired the
Argyll island from the MacQuarrie family. The tartan is
based on the black-and-white sett, sometimes
known as Clergy, suitable for ministers of religion.
Famous persons include George Rogers Clark
(1752–1818), pioneer of the American Midwest, and
General Mark Clark of the U.S. Army in World War II.

COCHRANE

Badge: A prancing horse, with the Latin
  motto *Virtute et labore* (By valor and
  hard work)

This clan claims descent from a Viking raider of the tenth century who settled in Renfrewshire, although the name is derived from Coveran near Paisley and in this form Waldeve de Coveran is noted in a charter of 1262, while William de Coveran was a signatory of the Ragman Rolls in 1296. William Blair (1605–86) married the Cochrane heiress and assumed the surname. He purchased the Dundonald estate in Ayrshire in 1638 and became the first earl in 1669. In the best tradition of their Viking ancestor, the "Fighting Cochranes" produced many men who rose to the highest ranks in the Army or Navy. Best known was Thomas, the tenth earl (1775–1860), one of the most brilliant seamen of the Napoleonic period. Convicted of fraud in 1814, he was expelled from Parliament, cashiered from the Navy, and sent to prison. On his release he went abroad, commanding the navies of Brazil, Peru, and Chile in their struggles for independence. He was also an advocate of screw propulsion and chemical warfare. Other famous persons of this name include the theatrical impresario Sir Charles Cochran and aviation pioneer Jacqueline Cochran.

COCKBURN

Badge: A cock crowing, with the Latin
    motto *Accendit cantu* (He is roused by
    cock crow)

The cock in the clan emblem is a misnomer, since the family derives its name from the lands of Cukoueburn (Cuckoo-burn) in Berwickshire. Around 1190, Peter de Cokburne was witness to a charter. Sir Alexander Cockburn was killed at Bannockburn in 1314, while his namesake and grandson was Keeper of the Great Seal in 1389–96. A later Sir Alexander was Lord Chief Justice of the United Kingdom in the nineteenth century, while many other members of the family rose to prominence in the law, politics, agriculture, and the armed services. The name is pronounced "Coburn," which is also a variant spelling. Members of the clan include the actors Charles Cockburn and James Coburn.

COLQUHOUN

Badge: A hart's head, with the French motto
    Si je puis (If I can)
Gaelic: *Mac a'Chombaich*

The clan takes its name from Colquhoun (pronounced "Cohoon") in Dunbartonshire, granted to Humphrey of Kilpatrick in the early thirteenth century. Subsequently, the estate of Luss on Loch Lomond was added by marriage. A feud between the Colquhouns and the MacGregors came to a head in 1603 when an attempt by the Colquhouns to ambush their enemies was forestalled. In the resulting battle at Glenfruin, the last armed confrontation between rival clans on the Scottish mainland, the Colquhouns were soundly beaten and their chief killed. As a result of charges laid against the MacGregors, that clan was proscribed, its lands seized, and even the very name expunged.

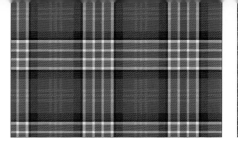 

COMMONWEALTH

The British Empire, which by 1940 covered a quarter of the world, gradually evolved into the Commonwealth of Nations. As long ago as the Imperial Conference of 1926, the term "Commonwealth" was coming into use, mainly in connection with the dominions, which had equal status with the mother country. This was given a legal definition in the Statute of Westminster in 1931. In 1957, the British Empire and Commonwealth Games were held in Wales but the following year the term "Empire" was formally dropped. Lochcarron designed this sett, using the red, white, and blue colors of the British flag. A variant of this, with white bands replacing the brown, was designed by L. P. G. Dow of Edinburgh in 1986 and was worn by officials and athletes taking part in the Commonwealth Games staged in Edinburgh that year. It has since become a universal, all-purpose tartan.

CONNEL

Badge: A boar's head between two wings
Gaelic: *Conall* (As powerful as a wolf) or
Comhngall (Fellow homage)

The name Connel or Connal is derived either from Comgall, a Celtic saint, founder of the abbey of Bangor, County Down, and contemporary of Columba, who accompanied him on his mission to convert the Picts in the late sixth century; or St. Congual, who preached the gospel in Galloway and Cumbria and gave his name to places as far afield as Dercongal in Dumfriesshire and Congleton in Cheshire. Three kings of Dalriada in the sixth century bore the names Congallus or Conall, and the place-name Connel Ferry, where Loch Etive enters the Firth of Lorne, is a reminder of this. The name Connel has a close affinity to the Irish names O'Connell and Connolly, illustrative of the ancient ties between Ireland and Scotland.

COOPER

Badge: A lion's jamb between two sprigs
of holly, with the Latin motto *Conata
perficio* (I perfect my undertakings)

As a surname, this can be traced back to the ancient trade of barrel-making, the term *cuparius* occurring in documents from the thirteenth century in medieval Latin. It also denotes a family origin, either Cupar in Fife or Coupar Angus in Perthshire. These names, as well as Cowper, are variants. Cupar may be small in terms of population, but it, rather than Kirkcaldy or St. Andrews, is the county town of Fife, a reminder that it was the ancient seat of the Thanes of Fife, who chose it for its geographical convenience. It became a seat of royal administration in the thirteenth century and a royal burgh a century later. Among the famous people of this name were the film actors Gary and Gladys, the comedian Tommy, the novelist James Fenimore, and the ceramic designer Susie Cooper. The poet William Cowper (1731–1800) traced his origins to the Cupar family.

CORONATION

This is a universal tartan, which, as its name suggests, originated as a commemorative sett, woven in honor of the coronation in 1936 of King George VI and Queen Elizabeth. It embodies the red, white, and blue colors of the British flag but the predominantly red ground suggests the Royal Stewart tartan. It was particularly appropriate because the new queen (youngest daughter of the Earl of Strathmore and Kinghorne) had Scottish antecedents and the future King George VI had worn the kilt since early boyhood. There is some controversy surrounding this tartan, as it may have been originally intended for the coronation of Edward VIII, who abdicated in December 1936 in order to marry Wallis Simpson. The coronation went ahead as planned in May 1937, the only difference being the change of monarch.

CRANSTOUN

Badge: A sleeping crane (bird) clutching a stone, with the motto "Thou shalt want ere I want"

This prominent Midlothian family takes its name from the barony of Cranstoun. The Norman mercenary Elfric de Cranston was cited in a twefth-century document pertaining to Holyrood Abbey. Thomas de Cranstoun acquired estates in Roxburghshire in the late fourteenth century. Despite Thomas Cranston's execution for high treason, his kinsman Sir John Cranstoun of Morrieston was given command of the Border defenses and raised to the peerage in 1609. The title has been in abeyance since 1869. The best-known holder of the surname was Miss Cranston, who commissioned Charles Rennie MacKintosh to design her chain of Glasgow tearooms at the beginning of the twentieth century.

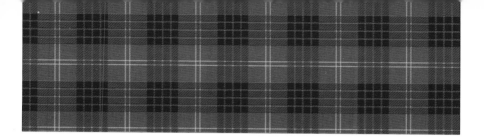

CRAWFORD

Badge: A stag's head surmounted by a
   cross, with the Latin motto *Tutum te
   robore reddam* (I will give you safety
   by strength)

Various prominent families with the surnames Crawford, Crawfurd, or Craufurd can trace their origins back to the ancient barony of Crawford in the Upper Ward of Lanarkshire, conferred on a Norman knight in the twelfth century. Crawfurds were hereditary sheriffs of Ayrshire and the mother of the patriot William Wallace belonged to this family. Her sister married David Lindsay, progenitor of the Earls of Crawford. Prominent branches of the clan to this day include the Crawfurds of Auchinames, and the Craufurds of Craufurdland and Kilbirnie, the latter producing a number of generals and ambassadors in the early nineteenth century. Famous Crawfords include the actor Michael Crawford and Thomas Crawford, sculptor of the Statue of Freedom atop the dome of the Capitol in Washington, D.C.

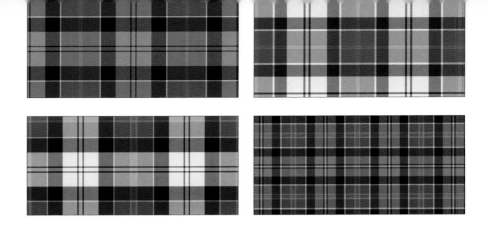

CULLODEN

This otherwise insignificant hamlet on the outskirts of Inverness would never have been known to the world at large had it not been the location of the last battle fought on British soil. It was here, on April 16, 1746, that the Jacobites under Prince Charles Edward Stuart were decisively defeated by the Hanoverian troops of the Duke of Cumberland and the cause of the Stuarts destroyed. Two and a half centuries of storytelling have romanticized the battle, though it was an appalling disaster that devastated the Highlands and distorted the facts,

especially in giving the impression of a struggle between Scots and English when, in fact, many Englishmen fought on the Jacobite side and more Scots probably served in the government forces than with the rebels. A dozen tartans (a sample of which are illustrated here) have been created in recent years with the generic name of Culloden, many of them apparently derived from actual plaids or kilts worn by combatants. There is no clan as such, but the Culloden tartans may be worn by anyone, especially those with Jacobite sympathies.

CUMBERNAULD

Badge: A chevron over a hunting horn, with the Scots motto "Daur and prosper"

Evidence that tartan is a living force and not something fossilized in ancient traditions is this district tartan, created by Frank Gordon of Condorrat in 1987 at the request of Cumbernauld Development Corporation, partly to celebrate the twentieth anniversary of the New Town and partly to publicize its achievements and prospects. In the immediate postwar years, the problem of overcrowding in Glasgow was solved by the creation of a ring of satellite towns, of which Cumbernauld in Stirlingshire was one of the first. It provided cheap housing in a green field setting and easy access to a wide range of industries. The site was designated in 1956, construction began in 1964, and the first phase was formally inaugurated by Princess Margaret in 1967.

CUMMING

Badge: A lion rampant holding a dagger, with the motto "Courage"
Gaelic: *Cuimean*

The clan is descended from the Cumins or Comyns (both forms are still in use), a powerful family in Badenoch whose progenitor was Robert de Comyn, governor of Northumberland after the Conquest; his grandson William was appointed Chancellor of Scotland by David I. The Comyns originally held lands in Roxburghshire, but by marriage they acquired estates in Badenoch and Buchan. The Black Comyn, one of the Guardians of Scotland in the 1290s, backed John Baliol and fell foul of Robert Bruce. His son John was stabbed to death by Bruce at Dumfries in 1306, the foul deed that triggered off the War of Independence. Famous clansmen include the actors Robert Cumming and Peggy Cummins.

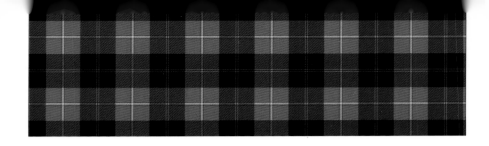

CUNNINGHAM

Badge: A unicorn's head, with the motto
"Over fork over"

Gaelic: *MacCuinneagain*

This family is of Norman origin and derives its name from the District of Cunninghame, one of the ancient baileries of Ayrshire. It was well established there in the mid-twelfth century but came to prominence at the Battle of Largs in 1263. By marriage, the chief acquired the lands of Glencairn, from which his descendant took his title when named an earl in 1488. The Y-shaped device on the arms of Marquess Conyngham (used as the emblem of the Cunninghame district) and the motto allude to an incident during the War of Independence when Robert Bruce was concealed from his pursuers by a Cunningham who forked straw over him as he lay in a cowshed. The fourteenth earl was the patron of Robert Burns, immortalized in a lament of 1791. With the death of the fifteenth earl five years later, the earldom became extinct. Famous clansmen include Robert "Don Roberto" Cunningham-Graham and the World War II naval commander Viscount Cunningham.

CURRIE

Gaelic: *Coire* (Corry) or *Mac Mhuirich* (Son of
    Murdoch)

This surname is borne by two quite distinct families. The first is a Lowland family, originating from Corrie, near Langholm, Dumfriesshire, and this variant is still common in that district. The spelling "Currie" is favored mainly in Arran and Ayrshire. The other family is from Argyll and the Isles and claims descent from Muireach O'Daly, a thirteenth-century harper to the King of Connaught, and he, in turn, claimed Niall of the Nine Hostages as his ancestor. Muireach's descendants settled in the Hebrides and held lands of the MacDonald Lords of the Isles in return for their services as clan bards. A variant of the surname is MacMurrich. This tartan was granted to the family of Currie of Balilone in 1822 by Lord MacDonald and is based on one of the MacDonald setts. Although originally a family tartan, it is now regarded as the tartan of Clan Currie. A second tartan, with red stripes, was designed by Lieutenant Colonel H. R. G. Currie and registered by the Clan Currie Association of Canada in 1981. Famous members of this clan include the nineteenth-century shipping magnate Donald Currie, the painter John Steuart Curry, and the Burns scholar James Currie.

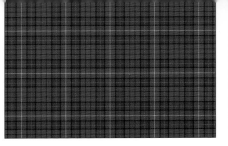 

DALMENY

Badge: A lion holding a primrose, with
   the Latin motto *Fide et fiducia* (By faith
   and trust)

This is one of the earliest district or territorial
tartans, recorded by Wilson's of Bannockburn
early in the nineteenth century. It pertains to the
picturesque village of Dalmeny, which forms part
of the estate of the Earls of Rosebery and lies
close to the approach to the Forth Road Bridge.
Its chief feature is the twelfth-century Norman
church, regarded as one of the finest of its kind
anywhere in Britain. It is first documented in 1296,
when Gilbert de Dunmanym put his name to the
Ragman Rolls.

DALZIEL

Badge: An upright dagger, with the motto
   "I dare"
Gaelic: *Dal geal* (White valley)

The surname, which is pronounced like the initials
"D. L.," comes from the barony of Dalzell in
Lanarkshire and has been in existence at least since
1288 when Hugh de Dalzell was sheriff of Lanark.
Sir Robert Dalzell was raised to the peerage in 1633
and became Earl of Carnwath six years later. On the
death of the fifth earl, the title passed to his
kinsman, Sir Robert Dalzell of Glenae. Best known
of this clan is the family of Dalyell of the Binns. Sir
Thomas Dalyell (1599–1685) rose to high rank in the
Russian army before serving as commander of the
Royalist forces in Scotland and raised the Royal
Scots Greys in 1681. His direct descendant and
namesake is Tam Dalyell, the radical member of
parliament.

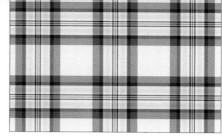

DAVIDSON

Badge: A stag's head, with the Latin motto
  Sapienter si sincere (Wisely if sincerely)
Gaelic: *MacDhaibhidh*

Because the pronunciation of the Gaelic name sounds rather like Mackay, there is an erroneous assumption that the two clans are connected. The progenitor of this clan was Black David of Invernahaven, fourth son of Muireach, Parson of Kingussie (1173), who founded the Clan MacPherson. From the founding father the clan came to be known as Clan Dhai, anglicized as Davidson. Intermarriage with the rival Mackintosh clan brought the Davidsons into the Clan Chattan confederacy in the early fourteenth century. The Davidsons became embroiled in the feud between the MacPhersons and Mackintoshes, and in the battle at the North Inch of Perth (1396), thirty men on either side were chosen to fight to the death.

DIANA

There are at least four tartans named in honor of Diana, Princess of Wales. Flairtex of Darvel created the Diana hunting tartan in 1981 to celebrate the marriage of the Lady Diana Spencer to the Prince of Wales and, like most hunting setts, it was a very somber tartan with rich royal purple stripes. It may also have been intended as an allusion to the fact that Diana was the Roman goddess of hunting. A dress version, with a characteristically lighter background, was also produced. Ironically, as her brother Earl Spencer said in her funeral oration, she became the most hunted person of the twentieth century and was killed in a car crash in Paris in August 1997. Lochcarron designed and manufactured this tartan, officially known as the Diana, Princess of Wales Memorial tartan, within days of her death. It was relaunched a year later by George Russell, chief executive of Scotland the Brand, as a fundraiser for the Diana Memorial Trust.

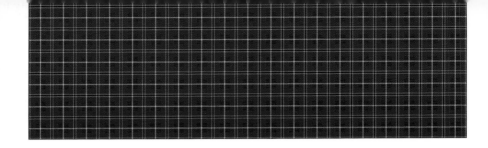

DOUGLAS

Badge: A salamander amid flames, on top
of a cap of maintenance, with the French
motto *Jamais arrière* (Never behind)

Gaelic: *Dubhghlas*

This powerful clan takes its name from a place in southern Lanarkshire meaning "black stream" and came to prominence during the War of Independence when the Black Douglas was Bruce's chief supporter. Over the ensuing centuries, the fortunes of this family have ebbed and flowed, marrying into the royal family a dozen times and holding the chief offices of state. From the Douglases stem the Earls, Marquesses, and Dukes of Queensberry, the Earls of Morton, and the Dukes of Douglas, although, as a result of deaths without issue, some of these titles passed to the Dukes of Buccleuch and Hamilton. Most notorious of the Queensberry branch were the second duke, who engineered the Union of 1707, the celebrated rake, known as "Old Q"; the marquess who devised the rules of boxing; and his younger son, Lord Alfred Douglas, the "Bosie," who played a shameful part in the downfall of Oscar Wilde.

DRUMMOND

Badge: A goshawk, with the motto
"Gang warily"

Gaelic: *Drummann*

The clan takes its name from Drymen, near Loch Lomond in Dunbartonshire, and traces its roots back to Maurice, Prince of Hungary, who escorted Princess Margaret, the future wife of Malcolm Canmore, to Scotland. Malcolm de Drymen supported Robert Bruce and is credited with the use of calthrops, the concealed spikes that crippled the English cavalry in the Bruce's battles. He was rewarded with estates in Perthshire. Successive Drummonds served the monarchy well and acquired many titles, including the earldom of Melfort and viscountcy of Strathallan. The senior line became Dukes of Perth, but this was a title forfeited after Culloden.

DUNBAR

Badge: A plumed horse's head, with the
Latin motto *Candoris praemium honos*
(Honor is the reward of integrity)

Gaelic: *Dùn bàrr* (Fort on the point or
headland)

The ancient fishing port and later holiday resort of Dunbar, on the coast of East Lothian, was made a royal burgh in 1369. Having been for a long time a place of strategic importance on the road to England, its chief family traced its origins from Crinan, the nephew of King Duncan, who was granted the estate by Malcolm III in 1072. Its castle played a prominent role in Scotland's turbulent history, notably in 1338 when Black Agnes, the redoubtable Countess of March and Dunbar, defended it against an English siege for six weeks during her husband's absence. Because of its extensive possessions in Moray, the Dunbar family was officially recognized as a Highland clan as long ago as 1579. Clan members include the poet William Dunbar, dubbed the "Scottish Chaucer," who flourished in the early sixteenth century, and his namesake (1749–1810), a native of Moray, who migrated to America and surveyed much of Texas, Arkansas, and Louisiana in 1804–05.

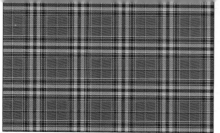

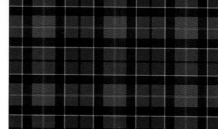

DUNBLANE

Badge: A crown over a chevron and a hand on one side, and a fess dividing lowes of flames, with the Latin motto *Renovate animus veritate* (Renew your courage with truth)
Gaelic: *Dùn blean*

This is both a district and a family tartan that is not untypical of many of the early nineteenth-century creations, when the vogue for tartan reached unprecedented heights. That the tartan is of considerable antiquity was borne out by a fine portrait of Peregrine, second Viscount Dunblane, in Highland dress, obviously predating his death in 1729. The painting served as the basis for the tartan woven in 1822 prior to the state visit of George IV to Scotland and has been in use ever since. The motto and right side of the arms refer to the martyrdom of St. Lawrence, who was roasted on a gridiron.

DUNCAN

Badge: A three-masted sailing ship, with the Latin motto *Disce pati* (Learn to suffer)
Gaelic: *Donnachaidh*

Originally a branch of the Robertsons, the clan traces its origins back to Donnachadh Reamhar (Fat Duncan), who led the clan at Bannockburn and tipped the balance in favor of Bruce. In later times, the Duncans held lands in Angus. Sir William Duncan was a physician to George III and created a baronet, but the most illustrious member of the family was Adam Duncan, who rose through the ranks of the Royal Navy and was named a viscount in recognition of his spectacular victory over the French and Dutch at Camperdown in 1797.

DUNDAS

Badge: A lion's head peering through an oak
     bush, with the French motto *Essayez* (Try)
Gaelic: *Dùn deas* (South fort)

The lands of Dundas in West Lothian were
conferred by Malcolm IV (1153–65) on Helias the
son of Uchtred, but the clan traces its ancestry to
Serle de Dundas a generation later. Later members
of the family played a prominent part in the Wars of
Independence, rewarded by further grants of land
in the fourteenth and fifteenth centuries. Sir James
Dundas, first Lord Arniston (1662), served as a
judge and started a long family tradition in the legal
profession, with several members becoming Lord
President of the Council. Most famous was Henry
Dundas (1742–1811), first Viscount Melville, known
as the uncrowned King of Scotland and nicknamed
Harry the Ninth.

DUNDEE

Badge: A pot of three lilies, with the Latin
     motto *Prudentia et candore* (With thought
     and purity)
Gaelic: *Dun-dè* (Tay fort)

In terms of population, Dundee ranks fourth in
Scotland. The site of a Roman camp, it was the
stronghold of Kenneth MacAlpin in the ninth
century during his campaign to defeat the Picts
and unify the kingdom. It has been a place of
strategic importance ever since and, more recently,
the northern end of the great Tay rail and road
bridges. Its district tartan was recorded by Wilson's
of Bannockburn in 1819, but is believed to be
much older and is very similar to the sett of a tartan
jacket believed to have been worn by Prince
Charles Edward Stuart at Culloden in 1746.

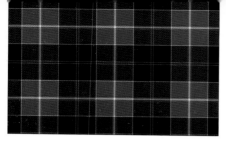

DUNLOP

Badge: A hand grasping a dagger, with the
    Latin motto *Merito* (By merit)
Gaelic: *Dùn lop*

This village in the Cunningham district of Ayrshire,
five miles northwest of Kilmarnock, has long been
famed for its cheeses. Its estate first appears in
documents in 1260 and in 1296 Neel FitzRobert de
Dullope signed the Ragman Rolls. The Dunlops of
Dunlop suffered forfeiture for supporting John
Balliol and later the Covenanters, but on both
occasions had their estates restored. Frances
Anna Wallace, who claimed descent from William
Wallace, married John Dunlop of Dunlop, and in
her widowhood she became the patron and chief
correspondent of Robert Burns. Her son James
was a general in the Peninsular campaign. Famous
members of the family include John Boyd Dunlop
(1840–1921), inventor of the pneumatic tire.

DUNOON

Badge: A three-towered castle surmounted
    by a galley, with the motto "Forward"
Gaelic: *Dùn Mhuin* (The stronghold of
    St. Mun)

As its name suggests, this resort on the Argyll coast
of the Firth of Clyde developed at the base of a hill
topped by a castle that dated back to the foundation
of the kingdom of Dalriada at the beginning of the
sixth century. Robert the Bruce appointed Sir Colin
Campbell of Loch Awe as constable, a hereditary
position held by the Dukes of Argyll to this day.
Dunoon's chief claim to fame was as the birthplace
of Margaret Campbell, Robert Burns's "Highland
Mary," whose statue occupies a prominent position
at the head of the pier. The Dunoon tartan was
designed by Harry Bayre in 1935 for the Glasgow
Irish pipe band, based in the town, so it is classified
as a corporate rather than a district tartan.

DURIE

DYCE

The name of Durie, a place near Scoonie in Fife, has all but vanished off the map, but its territorial tartan survives. Durie is first recorded in charters in 1238 when Duncan de Durry was a witness for the Earl of Strathearn. Other variants of the name include Doray and Dourie, but by the early sixteenth century the form had been standardized as Durie. The headship of the clan was in abeyance for many years, but in 1988 Lieutenant Colonel Raymond Durie of Durie was formally recognized and in this connection a tartan was created by Harry Lindsay. The sett has similarities to the tartan worn by the Argyll and Sutherland Highlanders, the regiment that Colonel Durie commanded.

The lands of Dyce near Aberdeen (the location of Aberdeen's airport since 1935) were in the possession of the family of this name from the middle of the fifteenth century, if not earlier. John de Diss was appointed a burgess of Aberdeen in 1467. The village itself boasts the ruins of an ancient church overlooking the Cothal Gorge, with two Pictish carved stones inserted in the east gable. In more recent years, Dyce has developed as a dormitory town for Aberdeen and has a wide range of light industries. The Dyce family has been prominent in the arts and include the Shakespearean scholar Alexander Dyce (1798–1869) and Sir William Dyce (1806–64), a painter, designer, and leading member of the Pre-Raphaelite group.

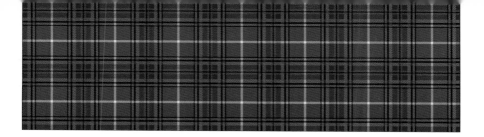

EDINBURGH

Badge: A triple-towered castle, with the Latin motto *Nisi Dominus frustra* (Unless the Lord wills it, it is in vain)

Gaelic: *Dun-éideann* (Edwin's burgh)

It was in 617 that Edwin, King of Northumbria, fortified the massive rock where the castle now stands. The houses that clung to the slopes of the rock developed into the Old Town, one of the most densely populated cities in Europe. With no room for lateral expansion, Edinburgh shot upward and boasted the world's first skyscrapers. It only became Scotland's capital in the mid-fifteenth century. The draining of the Nor' Loch in the eighteenth century eventually permitted the development of the New Town on a grid system, since copied in America and elsewhere. Several district tartans (including the Auld Reekie previously described) have been produced in relatively recent years in honor of Scotland's capital. This particular sett was designed by Hugh MacPherson in 1970 when Edinburgh hosted the Commonwealth Games (repeating the process in 1986). The colors are those of the civic arms and its two premier soccer teams, Hibernian and Heart of Midlothian.

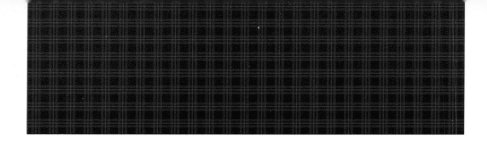

ELLIOT

Badge: An armed fist holding a broadsword,
with the Latin motto *Braviter et recte*
(Bravely and justly)

This clan was originally based in Forfar, although whether it derived its name from Eliot or gave its name to it is debatable. One school of thought maintains that the name comes from the Hebrew Elias. In 1395 the clan was persuaded to move to the Borders to defend Liddesdale from English incursions. Like the Armstrongs, they became one of the most powerful of the Border clans. Illustrious members of the clan include George Elliot of Stobs, who became governor of Gibraltar and withstood the four-year siege by France and Spain (1779–83), for which he was raised to the peerage as Lord Heathfield, Baron Gibraltar, in 1787. Gilbert Elliot was convicted of high treason (1685) but was later pardoned and became Lord Minto in 1705. His great-grandson was governor-general of India and named Earl of Minto in 1813. His aunt, Jane Elliot, composed the beautiful song with the title "The Flowers of the Forest."

ELPHINSTONE

Badge: A lady holding a tower and a laurel
  branch, with the motto *Cause causit*
  (Cause causes)

This family takes its name from the East Lothian village of Elphinstone, two miles south of Tranent. Nearby stands Elphinstone Tower, a fifteenth-century fortalice. A mansion was added in 1600 but demolished in 1865. Its chief claim to fame, or notoriety, is as the place where the Protestant leader George Wishart was imprisoned prior to his trial and burning at the stake in St. Andrews in 1546. It was the ancestral home of a family, which was in possession by 1235 when John de Elfinstun

appears in a charter. A century later, an Elphinstone married a niece of Robert the Bruce and from that time on they never looked back. The family provided many prominent figures throughout Scottish history. William Elphinstone (1431–1514) became Bishop of Aberdeen and Lord Chancellor, as well as founding King's College. In the seventeenth century the head of the clan was elevated to the peerage as Lord Balmerino. The last of the line was executed in 1746 for his part in the Jacobite Rebellion.

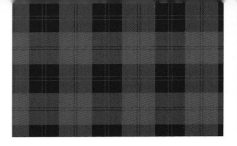

ERSKINE

Badge: A demi-lion rampant, with the Latin
motto *Decori decus addit avito* (He adds
honor to that of his ancestors)
Gaelic: *Arascain*

This clan takes its name from the barony of Erskine in Renfrewshire. Closely allied to Robert Bruce by marriage, Sir Robert de Erskine was Great Chamberlain of Scotland. From him are descended the Earls of Mar, Kellie, Buchan, and Rosslyn, whose ranks included the eleventh Earl of Mar, forfeited for his part in the Jacobite Rebellion of 1715; the poetic Earl of Buchan (a contemporary of Burns); and Thomas, Lord Erskine, who became Lord Chancellor. A brother of the Earl of Mar was Lord Grange, who had his wife Rachel abducted and marooned on the remote island of St. Kilda for several years, to prevent her from exposing a Jacobite plot.

EUROPEAN UNION

A unified Europe had been the dream of Napoleon and, later, Hitler, although in both cases it would have been a Europe subservient to either France or Germany. The desire to avoid conflict between the European countries led to the creation of the European Coal and Steel Community (France, Germany, Italy, and the Benelux states) in 1951. Out of this developed the European Common Market (1958), later the European Economic Community, and now the European Union, which embraces twenty-five countries (thirteen of which have adopted a common currency). The United Kingdom joined the EEC in 1973. The European Union tartan was designed by William Chalmers in 1998, the year in which the U.K. held the E.U. presidency. Its colors are those of the Scottish and E.U. flags, one with a white saltire cross and the other with twelve gold stars. It is intended for wear by any European Union citizen of Scottish descent.

FALKIRK

Badge: The church of Falkirk on a bend between six billets, with a shield and crossed claymores in the upper corner, and the Scots motto "Touch ane, touch a'" (Touch one, touch all)

Few towns in Scotland can boast such a colorful and turbulent history as Falkirk, which developed in the shadow of the Roman wall erected in 143. It was also the scene of major battles in 1298 and 1746, which sealed the respective fates of William Wallace and Bonnie Prince Charlie. From 1700 onward, it was the location of Scotland's largest cattle market and today boasts a wide range of industries. In 1990 the Falkirk District Council decided that it needed a tartan and consequently held a public competition. The prize-winning sett was designed by James McGeorge, who based it on a fragment of woolen checkered cloth known as the Falkirk Sett, which has been dated to the third century. The cloth was unearthed near the Antonine Wall, erected across the isthmus of the Forth and Clyde in the second century to keep the barbarian Caledonians at bay, and had been used to seal an earthenware jar. Thus one of the newest tartans can justifiably claim to be derived from the oldest.

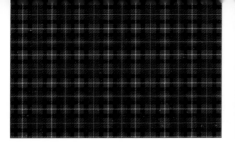 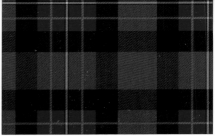

FARQUHARSON

Badge: A demi-lion rampant holding a
sword, with the Latin motto *Fide et
fortitudine* (By faith and fortitude)
Gaelic: *MacFhearchair*

This Aberdeenshire clan takes its name
from Farquhar, son of Shaw MacKintosh of
Rothiemurchus, who received the forfeited Comyn
lands in Braemar from Robert Bruce. Finlay Mor
carried the royal standard at Pinkie (1547). Ardent
supporters of the Stewarts, the Farquharsons
fought at Worcester (1651) and Preston (1715),
as well as at Falkirk and Culloden during the
last Jacobite Rebellion. Anne Farquharson of
Invercauld, known as "Colonel Anne," mobilized
the MacKintoshes for Prince Charlie, while her
husband fought on the opposing side.

FERGUSON

Badge: A crowned lion rampant issuing from
a crown, with the Gaelic motto *Clann
Fhearguis gu brath* (Clan Fergus forever)
Gaelic: *MacFhearghuis*

As Fergus is a common name, it is probable that
the people bearing this surname, or variants of it,
such as Fergus, Ferghie, MacFergus, and
Fergusson, now widespread throughout Scotland,
come from different roots. Families of this name
held lands in Aberdeenshire (Kinmundy and
Pitfour), Argyll (Strachur), Perthshire (Dunfallandy
and Balquhidder), Fife (Raith), Dumfries-shire
(Craigdrarroch), and Ayrshire (Kilkerran). The
Craigdarroch branch traces its origins to Fergus,
Prince of Galloway, in the twelfth century. Famous
clansmen include the poet Robert Fergusson. The
Kilkerran Fergusons have a long tradition of public
service, producing several Lords of Session.

FERGUSON OF BALQUHIDDER

The Perthshire district of Balquhidder at the eastern end of Loch Voil is renowned for the picturesque valley known as the Braes of Balquhidder. This district is chiefly associated with the exploits of the celebrated outlaw Rob Roy MacGregor, who, along with his feisty wife Helen and two of their sons, is buried near the ancient ruined church. While it was Rob Roy who put Balquhidder on the global tourist trail, the lands were historically associated with the small clan of MacLaren. Although the clan chief lost his lands at the beginning of the nineteenth century, the present chief acquired an estate in Balquhidder in the 1950s. The district is also associated with a branch of the Ferguson clan, whose tartan was recorded as early as 1831.

FIDDES

The ancient barony of Fiddes, sometimes spelled Fothos or Futhos, in Kincardineshire, has long since vanished into oblivion, but the name lingers on and people of this surname may be found all over the east coast of Scotland from Angus to Easter Ross and Cromarty. Eadmund de Fotheis, a landholder of Anglo-Saxon extraction, witnessed a charter in 1200. In 1289, Fergus de Fothes was enfeoffed of the "whole tenement" of Fothes by Alexander Comyn, Earl of Buchan. Many members of this clan entered the Church, from Sir William Fudes, Chancellor of Caithness, in 1524, to the Reverend Angus Fiddes, last ordained minister (and first postmaster) of lone St. Kilda.

FLETCHER

Badge: A demi-lion holding a cross, with the
Latin motto *Libertate extincta nulla virtus*
(Where liberty is dead, there is no valor)
Gaelic: *Mac an Fhleisteir*

This clan is unusual in that its name is derived from
a trade, the manufacture of arrows (from the
French word *flèche*). Traditionally, the Fletchers
were closely associated with the Campbells of
Argyll and claimed to have been the original
inhabitants of Glenorchy. The Fletchers of Glenlyon,
on the other hand, were arrowmakers to Clan
Gregor, while other important families of this name
were the Fletchers of Dunans and the Fletchers of
Innerpeffer, Angus, who acquired Saltoun in 1643.
Their most famous son was Andrew Fletcher
(1653–1716), the patriot who led the opposition to
the Union in 1707.

FORBES

Badge: A stag's head, with the motto "Grace
me guide"
Gaelic: *Foirbeis*

The progenitor of this clan was Duncan of Forbes,
who held the lands of that name in Aberdeenshire
from Alexander III in the thirteenth century. His son
Alexander was killed at the siege of Urquhart Castle
in 1304, while his son Alexander was slain at
Dupplin Moor in 1332. A much later Alexander,
Lord Pitsligo, opposed the Union and fought in the
rebellions of 1715 and 1745, for which his estates
were forfeited. Most famous of the family was
Duncan Forbes of Culloden, Lord President at the
time of the "Forty-five," who persuaded many of
the clans not to support the Stewart cause. In
Scotland the name is generally pronounced
"Forbs," but in Aberdeenshire it is pronounced
"Forb-es." Orville Fawbus was a clansman.

FORSYTH

Badge: A griffin segreant and armed, with the Latin motto *Instaurator ruinae* (A restorer of ruins)

Gaelic: *Fear sithe* (Man of peace)

Opinions are divided concerning the origin of this surname. The traditional view is that it is derived from Gaelic, implying that it was associated with ecclesiastics. More recent research suggests that it might have had a more prosaic origin, from Norman place-names such as Forsach or Frosnoc in the vicinity of Edinburgh, but which have vanished long since. The earliest reference to a person approximating to this name may be the Robert de Fauside, who signed the Ragman Rolls in 1296. Ten years later his son Osbert was given lands at Sauchie, Stirlingshire, by Robert the Bruce and fought at Bannockburn. Prominent members of the clan include William Forsyth (1737–1804), Chief Superintendent of the Royal Gardens, after whom forsythia (the floral emblem of the clan) is named; the filmmaker Bill Forsyth; and the novelist Frederick Forsyth.

FRASER

Badge: A buck's head, with the French
    motto *Je suis prest* (I am ready)
Gaelic: *Friseal*

The clan originated with a Norman mercenary whose name was either Fraise (strawberry) or Fraisier (strawberry plant). He settled in Tweeddale late in the eleventh century during the reign of Malcolm Canmore and had extensive estates in the Borders. Sir Andrew Fraser acquired the Lovat estates through marriage with a daughter of the Earl of Orkney. Simon Fraser, Lord Lovat, was "out" in 1715, but executed after the 1745–46 rebellion. His descendant raised the Lovat Scouts, which saw service in the Boer War and later British conflicts. Other clansmen include Simon Fraser, who explored the Fraser River in Canada, and Peter Fraser (1884–1950), Prime Minister of New Zealand (1940–49).

GALBRAITH

Badge: A muzzled boar's head, with the
    Latin motto *Ab obice suavior* (Sweeter
    for there having been difficulties).
Gaelic: *Clann a' Bhreatannaich* (The British
    family)

The Gaelic name suggests this clan was of Cymric stock from the ancient kingdom of Strathclyde, an independent region from the sixth century until 1018, whose inhabitants spoke a dialect of Brythonic (P-Celtic) akin to Welsh. The progenitor of the clan was Gilchrist Bretnach (the Briton). Sir William Galbraith was one of the regents of Scotland in the 1290s and his son Arthur was a staunch adherent of Robert the Bruce. Thomas Galbraith (1891–1985), descended from the Galbraiths of Blackhouse, Stirlingshire, was raised to the peerage in 1955 and took the title of Lord Strathclyde. (*See also* Russell and Hunter, which share the same tartan.)

GALLOWAY

Badge: A pelican on her nest, feeding her young with her own blood, with the Latin motto *Virescit vulnere virtus* (Courage gains strength from a wound)

Gaelic: *Gaillimh* (Land of foreigners)

The most southwesterly district of Scotland, barely twenty miles from Ireland and the Isle of Man, has very strong Hiberno-Norse affinities. Its Gaelic name is the same as that of Galway, the most westerly county of Ireland, and may have been applied to people who, for geographical reasons, seemed a race apart. In the case of the Gallovidians, this has been rationalized by the myths of Viking settlements or the last pocket of Pictish resistance to the Scots. In fact, the inhabitants of Galloway were listed in medieval royal charters as a separate people and spoke Gaelic long after the rest of the Lowlands was anglicized. The district tartan, however, dates back no further than 1950, when it was designed by John Hannay, a London chiropodist.

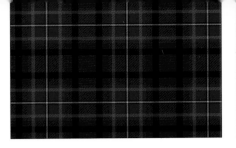 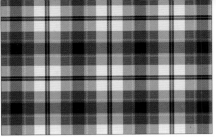

GILLIES

Gaelic: *Mac Gille Iosa* (Son of the servant of Jesus)

Like Clark, Gillespie, MacNab, MacTaggart, and Monk, this surname suggests an ecclesiastical origin and its variants include Gleason, Lees, MacAlees, MacLeish, and MacLise. As a forename it was popular with Clan MacPherson, but as a surname it occurs most frequently in the Badenoch district and the Outer Hebrides, especially the island of St. Kilda. Famous persons of this name include Sir William Gillies (1898–1973), president of the Royal Scottish Academy; Professor William Gillies, the chair of Celtic at Edinburgh University; his sister, the Gaelic singer Anne Lorne Gillies; the actor Jackie Gleason; the American poet and statesman Archibald MacLeish; Scotland's erstwhile First Minister Henry MacLeish; and the artist Daniel MacLise.

GLASGOW

Badge: A bell in a tree, with a salmon and a ring in its mouth, with the motto "Let Glasgow flourish"

Gaelic: *Glaschu* (The dear green place)

Scotland's largest city and at one time second city of the British Empire is the country's industrial capital, whose fortunes were built on the tobacco, sugar, and cotton trade with America before the Industrial Revolution made it the leading manufacturing center in the British Isles. Its phenomenal growth in the nineteenth and early twentieth centuries obscures the fact that it was an ancient ecclesiastical center founded and named by St. Mungo around 540, as well as the location of the fourth-oldest university in Britain (founded in 1451). The first of its many district tartans was recorded by Wilson's of Bannockburn in 1819.

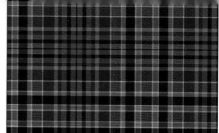

GORDON

Badge: A buck's head, with the Lowland
    Scots motto *Bydand* (Remaining)
Gaelic: *Gordon*

This powerful northern clan originated in the Borders, deriving its name from Gordon in Berwickshire, where a Norman progenitor held lands of David I. Sir Adam de Gordon undertook a diplomatic mission to the Pope in 1320, bearing a copy of the Declaration of Arbroath, and was rewarded by Robert Bruce with lands in Strathbogie. His descendant was named Earl of Huntly in 1449, and this became, successively, a marquessate (1599) and a dukedom (1684). In 1794 Jane, Duchess of Gordon, raised a regiment for the French war, rewarding each recruit with a kiss. Famous clansmen include George Gordon, Lord Byron, and General Charles "Chinese" Gordon, the heroic defender of Khartoum.

GORDON OF ABERGELDIE

Abergeldie Castle, on the south bank of the River Dee, about two miles east of the royal residence of Balmoral, was a residence of the Gordon clan from the early sixteenth century. The distinctive tartan, sometimes known as the Red Gordon, is a relatively modern creation, although it is derived from a tartan scarf worn by Rachel Gordon of Abergeldie, and shown in her portrait painted in 1723. This is but one of several major branches of the clan that have their own tartan. Others include the Gordons of Haddo, from whom descend the Earls of Aberdeen; the Gordons of Gight (whence came Lord Byron); the Gordons of Lochinvar, descended from Sir Adam of Gordon; and the Gordons of Strathbogie, who received their lands from Robert the Bruce.

GORDONSTOUN

The House of Plewlands on the Moray coast to the west of Lossiemouth changed its name to Gordonstoun in 1638 when it was acquired by Sir Robert Gordon. Almost three centuries later, it was purchased by Kurt Hahn (1886–1974), a leading German educationist who had fled from Nazi persecution in 1933 and opened the school a year later. Prince Philip had attended Hahn's school in Germany and as a result it was chosen for the education of Prince Charles. Hahn's theories, which emphasized physical rather than intellectual prowess, were also applied to the Outward Bound Schools (1941) and the Atlantic Colleges (1957). The remote location of Gordonstoun was ideally suited to the rugged education that the school offered. This is one of four tartans designed from 1956 onward and varying mainly in the yellow stripes. The version shown here is by Gordon Stewart, designed in 1966.

GOW

Badge: A thistle, with the Latin motto *Juncta arma decori* (Arms united to glory)
Gaelic: *Mac a'Ghobhainn* (Son of the smith)

As a trade surname, Gow is associated with several other clans, notably the MacPhersons, as a result of the blacksmith Hal o' the Wynd agreeing to make up the number of that clan at the battle of the North Inch in 1396. The Gows were chiefly to be found in Inverness-shire and Perthshire, and included the celebrated fiddlers Neil (1727–1807) and his son Nathaniel (1766–1831). The MacGowans, sometimes regarded as a separate clan, are mainly found in the central Lowlands and Dumfries-shire.

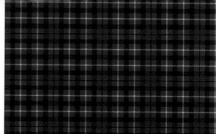

GRAHAM OF MENTEITH

Badge: A falcon proper, with the French
motto *N'oubliez* (Do not forget)
Gaelic: *Greumach*

The elder line of the Graham clan is descended from William de Graham, who witnessed a charter of Holyrood Abbey in 1128 and was granted the lands of Dalkeith by David I. His descendant, Sir Patrick Graham of Dundaff, married Euphemia, heiress of Prince David, Earl of Strathearn, son of King Robert II. In 1427 their son, Malise Graham, was robbed of his inheritance by James I, who conferred the lands and earldom of Strathearn on the boy's uncle, Robert Graham, the boy being pushed aside with the virtually meaningless title of Earl of Menteith instead. His descendant, however, became Earl of Airth and Menteith in 1633. The distinctive tartan of the Menteith branch of the clan has been in existence since at least 1816.

GRAHAM OF MONTROSE

Badge: An eagle preying on a stork, with the
French motto *N'oubliez* (Do not forget)
Gaelic: *Greumach*

One of the oldest clans, the name was well established by the early twelfth century when David I granted lands to William de Graham in Lothian. Grahams have played a prominent part in Scottish military history, from Sir John, killed under Wallace at Falkirk (1298), to Thomas, Lord Lynedoch (1750–1843), a hero of the Peninsular War. In between came Earls, Marquesses, and Dukes of Montrose, including the Great Marquess (executed in 1650) and the third duke, who was responsible for the repeal of the legislation prohibiting Highland dress. The present duke, long resident in Zimbabwe, was a leading supporter of Ian Smith's government.

GRAMPIAN

Badge: A cross-crosslet on a saltire cross,
  with no motto

This name is applied to a region of Scotland encompassing much of the northeast and taking its name from the massive range of mountains that dominates the landscape of Perthshire, Inverness-shire, and Aberdeenshire. A Scottish historian misread the name of a Roman victory at Mons Graupius, so strictly speaking the name should be the Graupian Mountains. The battle took place in A.D. 84 when the Romans under Agricola decisively defeated the Caledonians, although the actual site of the battle is unknown. The tartan is a trade tartan, one of many devised in very recent years. This tartan was designed by Polly Wittering for House of Edgar (Woollens) Limited of Perth, the colors symbolizing the blue sky, the purple heather, and the rich green countryside.

GRANT

Badge: An inflamed mountain, with the
  motto "Stand fast"
Gaelic: *Grannd*

Although it is sometimes asserted that the name derives from the Gaelic word *granda* (ugly), it is pure French, meaning "large" or "eminent," and testifies to the Norman origin of the clan, where the French equivalent of the motto "Stand fast" was in use before 1066. It may be that a scion of this family married a Siol Alpin (the seed of Alpin) heiress, who could trace her roots back to the tenth century, but in Scotland the Grants first appear as sheriffs of Inverness in the thirteenth century. Lawrence Grant married a Comyn heiress and acquired Strathspey, the district most associated with the clan to this day. Ulysses S. Grant, commander of the Union armies in the U.S. Civil War and seventeenth president (1868–76), is probably the most famous clansman.

GRANT OF MONYMUSK

Badge: The sun shining on a tree trunk, with
the Latin motto *Te favente virebo* (Under
your favor, I will flourish)

Gaelic: *Grannd*

The village and parish of Monymusk in Aberdeenshire has ancient ecclesiastical connections, including one of the finest Norman churches in Scotland and the remains of an Augustinian priory that was erected on the site of a Culdee settlement dating to the sixth century. A casket containing relics of St. Columba, formerly borne before the Scots in battle, was in the care of Malcolm de Monymusk in 1315 and for many centuries was preserved in Monymusk House before its transfer to the National Museum of Antiquities in Edinburgh. The tartan worn by the Grants of Monymusk is only one of at least sixteen Grant tartans, which include hunting and dress tartans for general clan use, as well as the distinctive setts associated with such families as the Grants of Ballindalloch, Corriemony, Glenmorriston, Rothiemurchus, and Tullochgorum.

GUNN

Badge: A right hand wielding a broadsword,
with the Latin motto *Aut pax aut bellum*
(Either peace or war)

Gaelic: *Guinne*

Although this clan claims descent from Gunni, son
of Olaf the Black, Norse King of Man and the Isles
in the twelfth century, it is now believed that it is
derived from a Pictish tribe inhabiting Caithness a
thousand years earlier. Extremely warlike and
unruly, the clan was forced to migrate southward
and resettle in Sutherland in the fifteenth century.
George Gunn the Crowner (a hereditary legal
appointment) was the father of many sons, each of
whom was the progenitor of families that are now
septs of the clan.

GUTHRIE

Badge: A right hand wielding a sword, with
the Latin motto *Sto pro veritate* (I stand
for truth)

This is one of the clans that derives its name from a
Norse ancestor, Gudrum or Guthrum, anglicized
originally as Gutherin and applied to lands in Tayside.
The village of Guthrie, seven miles east of Forfar, was
originally attached to Arbroath Abbey, while nearby
Guthrie Castle dates from the late fifteenth century.
A Guthrie was the Scottish emissary sent to France
in 1299 to recall William Wallace from his diplomatic
mission to enlist the aid of the Continental powers in
the struggle against Edward of England. Sir David
Guthrie was Lord Treasurer of Scotland from
1461–67 and was rewarded by permission to erect
the castle. Clan members include the pioneer of
anaesthesia, Samuel Guthrie (1782–1848), and the
director Tyrone Guthrie (1900–71).

HAIG

Badge: A cluster of rocks, with the motto
"Tyde what may"

The motto comes from a prophecy of Thomas the Rhymer, the medieval soothsayer: "Tyde what may, whate'er betyde, Haig shall be Haig of Bemersyde." It alluded to a family who had been lairds of Bemersyde in the Borders since the twelfth century, but when Sophia Haig, the twenty-seventh Laird, died unmarried in 1878, the estate passed to a cousin. In 1921 he sold it so that it could be presented by a grateful nation to Field Marshal Earl Haig (1861–1928), a distant kinsman of the seventeenth Laird, who became the twenty-ninth Laird of Bemersyde. At that time Earl Haig adopted as his tartan the black, blue, and white check, previously known as the Buccleuch or Gladstone check, which was worn by the local regiment, the King's Own Scottish Borderers. Haig had served in the cavalry (Seventh Hussars) before joining the General Staff and never actually wore the kilt during his military service, contrary to popular belief.

HAMILTON

Badge: An oak tree on a ducal coronet, with the motto "Through"

Gaelic: *Hamultun*

Like the Barclays, this clan derives its name from a place in England—Hambledon in the Thames Valley—which the Norman progenitor held. Half a century later, the first of the family to head north arrived in Scotland and from him was descended Walter Fitz Gilbert, governor of Bothwell Castle at the end of the thirteenth century. Changing sides, he was rewarded by Robert Bruce with the barony of Cadzow in Lanarkshire, from which the Hamilton estates expanded in the ensuing centuries. James,

sixth of Cadzow, was named Lord Hamilton in 1445, but his son James became Earl of Arran in 1503 and Duke of Chatelherault (France) in 1549. Eventually the head of this powerful family held three dukedoms, adding Hamilton (1643) and Brandon in England. A grandson of the second Earl of Arran became Earl of Abercorn (1606) and descendants became Marquess (1790) and Duke (1868). The Earls of Haddington originate from a junior branch.

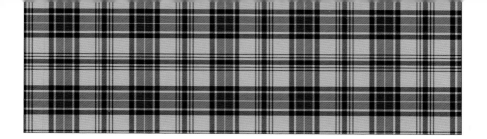

HANNAY

Badge: A cross-crosslet fitchee issuing out of a crescent, with the Latin motto *Per ardua ad alta* (Through difficulties to higher things)

Gaelic: *Ui hAnnaidh* or *Ap Shenaigh*

From the Goidelic (Irish) and Brythonic (Welsh) versions given above came the anglicized form Ahannay, the name borne by this very old Celtic family in Galloway. The Ragman Rolls record Gilbert de Hannethe, who acquired the lands of Sorbie, Wigtownshire, and this remained the family stronghold until the seventeenth century, when they came off worse in a deadly feud with the Murrays of Broughton and were outlawed and dispossessed.

Cadet branches of the clan, however, acquired estates at Kirkdale and Mochrum and the surname is still very common in Galloway. The family includes the soldier-poet Patrick Hannay and James Hannay, the dean of St. Giles attacked by Jenny Geddes in July 1637 for attempting to recite the new Episcopal liturgy that triggered off the first of the religious wars. Both Hanna and Hannah are variants of the name.

HAY

Badge: A falcon with outstretched wings, with the Latin motto *Serva jugum* (Save the yoke)

Gaelic: *Mac Garaidh*

Another of the Norman families, which came to Scotland in the twelfth century, the Hays trace their origins to William de la Haye, cupbearer to Malcolm IV. His eldest son, William, was the progenitor of the Earls of Errol, while his second son, Robert, was the ancestor of the Hays of Yester, who later gained the marquessate of Tweeddale. In 1314, Gilbert de la Haye was confirmed as hereditary High Constable of Scotland under Robert Bruce and this office has ever since been held by successive Earls of Errol, taking precedence over all other hereditary honors after the Blood Royal. The Earls of Kinnoul are an offshoot from the Hays of Errol. The name comes from the French word *hail* (hedge), hence the Gaelic equivalent *garadh*.

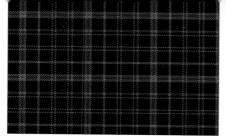 

HEBRIDEAN

Martin Martin of Dunvegan, Skye, who toured the Outer Hebrides extensively in the late seventeenth century, noted that the tartans worn by the people of Lewis, Harris, the Uists, Benbecula, and Barra differed from island to island rather than from clan to clan, and it seems likely that many of the so-called family tartans of a later generation had territorial rather than clan origins. The wheel has come full circle in recent years with the development of the district tartans, and therefore it is singularly appropriate that some of these pertain to the islands. There are several ancient tartans, those from North and South Uist being particularly distinctive. Paradoxically, the Hebridean tartans are rarely worn in the islands themselves, for the simple reason that most inhabitants have a clan tartan and this is generally preferred.

HENDERSON

Badge: A hand holding a five-pointed star surmounted by a crescent, with the Latin motto *Sola virtus nobilitat* (Valor alone ennobles)
Gaelic: *Mac Eanruig*

This name, meaning son of Henry, gives rise to such variants as Henryson, Hendry, and MacKendrick. Another variant, Eanrick, is regarded as a sept of Clan Gunn, descended from Henry, son of George the Crowner. The main clan, however, originated in Glencoe. A daughter of the Henderson chief married Iain MacDonald, brother of the first Lord of the Isles, and from them were descended the MacLain MacDonalds of Glencoe, massacred by the Campbells in 1692. Alexander Henderson (1583–1646) was a celebrated churchman who drafted the National Covenant (1638) and the Solemn League and Covenant (1643).

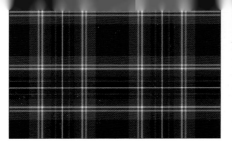

HOLYROOD

HOME

The Palace of Holyroodhouse, the sovereign's official residence in Scotland, takes its name from the ancient Abbey of the Holy Rood, whose ruins provided a sanctuary for debtors until 1880. Ironically, Sir Walter Scott, when he was faced with ruin and bankruptcy, even contemplated fleeing there, but he weathered the storm, redoubled his efforts as a writer, and went on to become the impresario of the Royal Visit of 1822. The Holyrood tartan was designed by Lochcarron Weavers in 1977 to celebrate the Queen's Silver Jubilee, but it did not receive official sanction, so the company simply renamed it Holyrood and marketed it all the same. What started out as a commemorative tartan has since become one of the all-purpose or trade tartans. Holyrood is second only to Edinburgh Castle as Scotland's leading tourist attraction.

Badge: A lion's head on a cap of
  maintenance, with the motto
  "A home, a home, a home"
Gaelic: *Uamh* (Cave)

This name is pronounced "Hume" (and often spelled like that) and derives from a place in Berwickshire that was settled by descendants of Earl Gospatrick of Northumbria in the thirteenth century. By marriage and clan foray the Homes became one of the most powerful Border families. Distinguished clansmen include the Earls of Home, the philosopher David Hume (1711–76), and the playwright John Home. The fourteenth earl renounced his title and, as Sir Alec Douglas-Home, was British Prime Minister in 1963–64, but later returned to the House of Lords as Baron Home of the Hirsel.

HOOD, ROBIN

It is perhaps not surprising that this tartan is more commonly known nowadays as the Rob Roy hunting tartan, the confusion between one legendary outlaw and another being understandable. The simple pattern of black and Lincoln green was created by Wilson's of Bannockburn in 1819 to cash in on the popularity of the character in Scott's romance *Ivanhoe*, published that year. There are myths and place-names associated with Robin Hood all over England, but he really existed and is recorded in a pipe roll of 1230 relating to Yorkshire as "Robertus Hood fugitivus." The outlaw first appears in literature in *Piers Plowman* (c. 1360), though significantly, he also features in Wyntoun's *Chronicle of Scotland* (1420), which included details of his exploits. Historians now agree that he was born Robert Fitz-ooth (Fitz-hugh) at Locksley in Nottinghamshire around 1160 of good Norman stock and connected to the Earl of Huntingdon.

HOPE

Badge: A broken terrestrial globe, with the
Latin motto *At spes infracta* (But hope
is unbroken)

This family held extensive lands in the vicinity of
Edinburgh for centuries. John de Hop is listed in
the Ragman Rolls of 1296 while Sir Simon de la
Hope features in a charter of 1321. Sir Thomas
Hope (1580–1646) rose to prominence in the reign
of James VI, amassed a fortune, and purchased
the estates of Edmonston, Prestongrange, and
Craighall. From his youngest son Sir James
(1614–61) sprang the first Earl of Hopetoun, who
commissioned the building of Hopetoun House
between 1699 and 1703. Many members of the
clan became prominent in the law, politics, and
banking. Famous persons of this name include the
novelist Sir Anthony Hope (author of *The Prisoner
of Zenda*), and the comedian Bob Hope.

HOUSTON

Pronounced "Hooston" in Scotland, this village and
parish of the same name in Renfrewshire is derived
from "Hugh's tun" (farmstead). In turn, it gives rise
to the surname, which is still quite common in that
county. Members of this family held lands in
Renfrewshire and Lanarkshire from the twelfth
century and it was a lady of this family who gave
her name to the Glasgow district of Bellahouston.
The name is better known in America (where it is
pronounced more closely to its original derivation
as "Hyooston"). Prominent members of the family
include the New Zealand pianist Michael Houston,
the singer and actress Whitney Houston, and Sam
Houston, president of Texas (1836–45) and later its
first governor, after whom the city of Houston is
named. The tartan was jointly commissioned in
1994 by J. P. Houston of Arkansas and W. J.
Houston of New Zealand for the benefit of
Houstons everywhere.

HUNTER

Badge: A seated greyhound, with the Latin motto *Cursum perficio* (I accomplish the hunt)

This is a trade name, originally applied as an epithet to a huntsman and therefore found all over Scotland. The Hunters of Hunterston claim descent from the huntsman to Duke William of Normandy and it is believed that members of this family migrated to Scotland in the reign of David I. They held lands in Ayrshire from the early thirteenth century and received a charter of confirmation in 1375, subsequently holding the position of hereditary royal foresters in Arran and Cumbrae. Mungo Hunter of Hunterston was killed at the battle of Pinkie in 1547. Among his descendants were the brothers William (1718–83) and James (1728–93), both prominent surgeons in the reign of George III. William bequeathed his collections of coins, paintings, antiquities, and anatomical specimens to the University of Glasgow, which is the nucleus of the Hunterian Museum. The tartan shown here is the same as Galbraith and Russell. It was first known as Galbraith in the collection of the Highland Society of London, but William Wilson and Sons of Bannockburn recorded the pattern as Russell in their pattern book of 1847, although it was named Hunter in an earlier book of 1819.

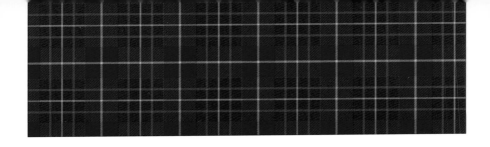

INGLIS

Badge: A demi-lion holding a mullet, with
the Latin motto *Recte faciendo securus*
(Sure in doing the right thing)

Just as Wallace and Vallence mean "Welshman," so Inglis is merely the Scots word for "Englishman." As a distinguishing epithet, it occurs in documents as far back as the middle of the twelfth century, originally in the Borders but later more widespread throughout the Lowlands. It is believed that many of these men were asylum-seekers who fled northward in the aftermath of the Norman Conquest, although by the thirteenth century the name was often applied to people who spoke English rather than Gaelic. The most prominent landowners of this name were the Inglis family of Cramond on the outskirts of Edinburgh, but others held land in Roxburghshire and Peebles-shire. Other famous persons of this name are Admiral Charles Inglis (1731–91), General Sir William Inglis (1764–1835), and John Inglis (1810–91), Lord Justice-General of Scotland, who was raised to the peerage in 1867 as Lord Glencorse.

INNES

Badge: A boar's head, with the Scots motto *Be traist* (Be faithful)

Gaelic: *Inis*

This clan traces its ancestry to Berowald, a Flemish mercenary in the service of Malcolm IV, from whom he received the lands of Innes in Moray in 1154. Berowald's grandson took Innes as his surname and was confirmed in his estates by Alexander II in 1226. The Gaelic word *inis*, from which the name is derived, merely means "islet" (anglicized as "inch"). Sir Robert Innes acquired the estates of Aberchirder by marriage in the fourteenth century, while his descendant of the same name received a baronetcy from James VI in 1625. Following the death of the fourth Duke of Roxburghe without issue, Sir James Innes in 1812 successfully petitioned the House of Lords for the Scottish titles and lands, and became the fifth duke. James, the sixth duke, was named Earl Innes in 1838. A cadet branch, the Inneses of Innermarkie, acquired a baronetcy from Charles I in 1631 for services to the Stewart cause.

INVERNESS

Badge: Christ on the cross, flanked by an elephant and a camel

Gaelic: *Inbhir Nis* (Mouth of the River Ness)

The ancient capital of Pictland, and the Highlands in more recent years, Inverness was raised to the dignity of a city in 2001. It was here that St. Columba converted King Brude to Christianity in the sixth century, but the tale of MacBeth murdering King Duncan there is a myth perpetuated by Shakespeare. There was a medieval castle overlooking the Ness in the past, but the present red sandstone structure is Victorian. Inverness boasts half a dozen distinctive tartans, several of which were designed in the 1790s and early 1800s for the local fencible regiments, the Inverness Militia and the Inverness Highland Rifle Volunteers. The tartan illustrated here, however, was designed around 1820 for Augustus, Earl of Inverness, but subsequently regarded as the burgh tartan.

IRVINE

Badge: A sheaf of holly, with the Latin motto
Sub sole sub umbra virens (Flourishing in
sunshine and shade)

This very ancient family traces its ancestry to Duncan Eryvine (around 965), a descendant of the Kings of Dalriada, whose eldest son acquired the lands of Bonshaw in Dumfriesshire. His descendant William de Irwin was a near neighbor of the Bruces of Annandale and became armor-bearer to Robert the Bruce. Irvines are in Bonshaw to this day; one of them, Sir Robert Irvine, was the Commodore of the *Queen Mary*. Other branches of the family became Lairds of Drum in Aberdeenshire and rose to prominence in the northeast. The variant spelling Irving is also common from Dumfriesshire to Orkney, whence came the surname for preacher Edward Irving, the celebrated actor Sir Henry Irving, and the American novelist Washington Irving. Most famous of the present-day Irvines is the Lord Chancellor, Lord Irvine of Lairg.

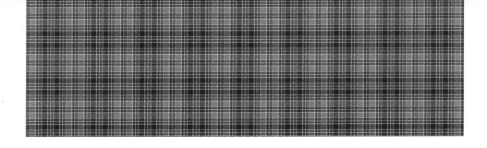

JACOBITE

Badge: A white rose

The term "Jacobite" was applied to followers of King James VII and II and his descendants who fought against William of Orange, and later the first two Georges, in a bid to restore the ancient Stuart dynasty to the throne. The term has often become synonymous with the Scottish Highlands, although the Jacobites included many Lowland Scots, Irishmen, and Englishmen in their ranks, while many Highlanders fought just as resolutely for the other side. Even before the uprising, known as the first Jacobite Rebellion (1715), sympathy for the old regime gathered momentum after the Union in 1707, and it became fashionable for Stuart partisans to wear a white cockade in their hats and scarves or sashes of tartan. One of these, dating from 1712, is believed to have been the source of the Jacobite tartan worn during the rebellions of 1715 and 1745–46. Like all other tartans, it was banned from then until 1782, but it gradually returned to favor in the ensuing half century as the romance of Jacobitism superseded the reality, and is now regarded as one of the all-purpose tartans.

JARDINE

Badge: A six-pointed spur rowel, with the
Latin motto *Cave adsum* (Look out, I
am here)

The name of this prominent Border clan is derived from the French word *jardin* (garden), and the du Jardin family came to England with the Conqueror in 1066. Like many other Norman mercenaries, they migrated to Scotland in the twelfth century and by 1150 the name crops up in various documents, either as "de Jardin" or Latinized as "de Gardinus." The principal line has held the lands of Applegirth, Dumfriesshire, since the fourteenth century. The Jardines played a notable part in the commercial development of the British Empire. Frank Jardine married a Samoan princess and developed Queensland and Northern Australia, while Dr. William Jardine, a surgeon of the East India Company, formed a partnership with James Matheson that dominated the China trade. Today, Jardine Matheson is known as a multinational conglomerate.

JOHNSTON

KEITH

Badge: A phoenix rising from the flames,
   with the Latin motto *Vive ut postia vivas*
   (Live that you may live hereafter)
Gaelic: *Maclain*

Badge: A stag's head, with the Latin motto
   Veritas vincit (Truth conquers)
Gaelic: *Ceiteach*

The name of this powerful Border clan comes from John's toun, the fortified dwelling of the chief who held lands in Annandale under the forebears of King Robert Bruce. Sir James Johnston was raised to the peerage in 1631 as Lord Johnston of Lochwood, and promoted a decade later to Earl of Hartfell. The second earl became Earl of Annandale in 1672, and his son became Marquess in 1701. The title became dormant in 1792, but Patrick Hope-Johnston of Westerhall successfully petitioned in 1986 for the revival of the title of Earl of Annandale and Hartfell. The Johnstons of Westerhall were descended from the same stock and became Baronets of Nova Scotia in 1700.

This important branch of Clan Chattan takes its name from Keith in Banffshire. A fourteenth-century marriage of the chief to the heiress of the Cheynes of Ackergill gave the Keiths extensive estates in Caithness, which brought them into a long-running conflict with the Gunns. The clan chief was hereditary Grand Marischal of Scotland, the fifth Earl Marischal founding the university college of that name in Aberdeen. The tenth earl was one of the leaders of the 1715 Jacobite Rebellion and was attainted as a result. His brother James had an illustrious career in the army of the Czar before reorganizing the Prussian army and becoming a field marshal under Frederick the Great.

KENNEDY

Badge: A swimming dolphin, with the French motto *Avise la fin* (Consider the end)

Gaelic: *Ceannaideach* (Ugly head)

Although the Gaelic name simply means "ugly head," it has been suggested that it is actually derived from *cinneadh* (kinsman), alluding to the fact that the progenitor of the clan, Henry, was a brother of William the Lion. The Kennedys first came to prominence in the late thirteenth century as supporters of the Bruces against the Comyns, and acquired lands of Cassilis in Carrick. The grandson of Mary Kennedy and King Robert III was the first Earl of Cassilis. Archibald, the twelfth earl, was named Marquess of Ailsa in 1831. The outlaw Ulric Kennedy fled from Carrick and settled in Lochaber, forming the sept of MacWalrick. Culzean Castle (now a Scottish National Trust property) had close associations with Dwight D. Eisenhower when he was Supreme Commander of the Allied Forces in World War II. It should be noted that the Irish Kennedys are a completely different tribe.

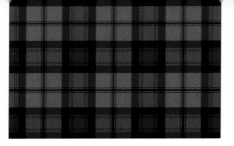

KERR

Badge: A radiate sun, with the Latin motto
   Sero sed serio (Late but serious)
Gaelic: *Cearr* or *MacGhillechearr*

Two Anglo-Norman brothers who settled in
Roxburghshire in the twelfth century were the
ancestors of this numerous clan that, by the
fourteenth century, had also established branches
in Ayrshire and Aberdeenshire. The Kers of
Cessford were wardens of the marches and
hereditary sheriffs of Roxburghshire, and from them
were descended the Lords, Earls (from 1616), and
Dukes (from 1707) of Roxburghe. From a cadet
branch, the Kers of Newbattle and Ferniehirst,
sprang the Earls of Ancrum and Marquesses of
Lothian. The most famous clansman was the
actress Deborah Kerr, who pronounced her name
"car" in the traditional manner.

KILGOUR

Gaelic: *Cille gobhar* (Cell or hermitage of the
   goat)

Regarded as a sept of the MacDuff clan, the
Kilgour family derives their surname from lands
near Falkland settled on them by the Thanes and,
later, Earls of Fife. By 1528 Sir Thomas Kilgour was
recorded as Chaplain to the King at Falkland
Palace (it should be noted that in this context the
title "Sir" was, at that time, used by clergymen as
well as knights), and he may well be the Thomas
Kingoure awarded a pension in 1567. The surname
is widespread but mainly associated with Fife and
Aberdeenshire, in whose records it occurs
frequently from the mid-sixteenth century onward.
In the 1850s a large number of Kilgours left
Scotland and immigrated to northern Australia,
their memory perpetuated in the Kilgour River in
Queensland. A variant is the surname Gower.

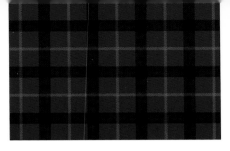

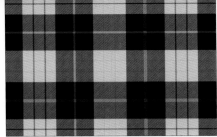

KINCAID

Badge: A triple-towered castle from which
   issues a dexter arm brandishing a sword,
   with the motto "This I'll defend"
Gaelic: *Ceann cadha* (Steep place)

This clan takes its name from the lands of Kincaid
in the foothills of the Campsies north of Glasgow,
which they held from the Earls of Lennox from the
early thirteenth century at least. The clan emblem
alludes to the heroic actions of the Laird of Kincaid,
who, as Constable of Edinburgh Castle, played a
prominent part in the Wars of Independence. As
well as extensive estates in western Stirlingshire,
the Kincaids held lands near Falkirk and Edinburgh
in the sixteenth and seventeenth centuries, notably
Blackness Castle, which served as a prison for
Covenanters during the religious wars. Staunch
Jacobites, the Kincaids chose exile after 1715 and
many of them settled in America.

KINNISON

Gaelic: *Mac Conan* or *Mac Conich* (Son of
   Conan)

Variants of the surname, derived from the Gaelic,
include Kinnieson, Cunnison, Cunieson, and
MacConich, and all are regarded as septs of the
MacFarlanes. The progenitor of the family is
believed to have been Conan de Glenerochy, a
bastard son of Henry, Earl of Atholl. The family held
lands of the Earls of Atholl at Edradour in the
vicinity of Pitlochry, famous for its distillery, which is
believed to be the smallest in Scotland, and there
are copious references to the lairds of Edradour
under various spellings of their surname, from
Cunyson to Cwnyson, in documents from the mid-
fifteenth century onward.

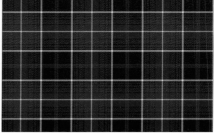

LAMONT

LARGS

Badge: An open right hand, with the Latin
   motto *Ne parcas nec spernas* (Neither
   spare nor dispose)
Gaelic: *MacLaomainn*

Rather confusingly, this powerful Argyll clan was at
one time known as the Clan Farquhar
(MacFhearchair) from an ancestor who lived long
before the emergence of the Farquharsons of
Aberdeenshire and with whom they had no
connection. By the early thirteenth century,
however, the chief of the clan had obtained a
hereditary judgeship, hence the name "lawman"
(laomann), from which the present name is derived.
The Lamonts clashed often with the Campbells,
who massacred over 200 of the clan at Dunoon in
1646. This atrocity was one of the crimes for which
the Marquess of Argyll was executed in 1661. It is
pronounced with the stress on the first syllable.

Badge: Three thistles over a Viking ship with
   the Norwegian lion on its sail
Gaelic: *Leargaidh Ghallda* (The foreign coast)

The seaside resort on the Clyde coast of North
Ayrshire sprang to fame in October 1263 when the
Scots, under Alexander III, defeated the Norse
armada of King Haakon V, an event commemorated
by the Pencil, a monument in the form of a Celtic
tower near the shore. It was a defining moment in
Scottish history, for it ended Viking supremacy and
resulted in the cession of the Hebrides and Kintyre to
Scotland three years later. Not surprisingly, the town's
chief tourist attraction is Vikingar, an exhibition that
vividly re-creates the Norse period. Elements of
Scandinavian colors dominate the district tartan,
which was commissioned by the district council and
designed by Sidney Samuels in 1981. There is also a
variant spelling, Larg.

LAUDER

Badge: A sentinel above a tower, with the
    Latin motto *Turris prudentia custos*
    (Prudence is the guardian of the tower)

This family of Norman origin takes its name from the village of Berwickshire, where they settled in the reign of Malcolm Canmore. William de Lawdere was sheriff of Perth in the reign of Alexander III and during the Wars of Independence a Lauder was the constable of the Bass Rock. Sir Robert Lauder became Justiciar under Robert the Bruce, while William Lauder was Chancellor of Scotland. John Lauder became Baronet of Fountainhall in 1690. The fifth baronet married Isobel Dick and the name of the chief family became hyphenated. Sir Thomas Dick-Lauder (1784–1848) was a well-known antiquary and philanthropist who collaborated with the Sobieski Stuarts in the compilation of *Vestiarium Scoticum,* their encyclopedia on tartan.

LEASK

Despite a long-running controversy regarding the origin of this name, it seems certain that it derives from lands in Aberdeenshire. William de Laskereske, who signed the Ragman Rolls in 1296, is sometimes regarded as the first of this name on record, although this has been cast into doubt, and the earliest positive documented use of the name occurs in a document dated to around 1345, confirming the grant of the lands of Leskgaranne to William Leask. At around that time, members of the family moved to Orkney, where the surname is common to this day, although often spelled Lask. The Leask tartan was created recently, in 1981.

LENNOX

Badge: Two broadswords crossed behind a swan's head and neck, with the motto "I'll defend"

Gaelic: *Lebhenach* (Smooth stream)

Members of this ancient Celtic family were the mormaers of the Lennox, a district encompassing modern Dunbartonshire together with parts of Renfrewshire, Stirlingshire, and Perthshire. By the late thirteenth century the Earl of Lennox was one of the most influential of the Scottish nobles, the family being staunch supporters of Robert the Bruce. Their power increased as a result of intermarriage with the royal Stewarts. Henry Stewart, Lord Darnley, younger son of the Earl of Lennox, was the ill-fated second husband of Mary, Queen of Scots, while his kinsman Esmé Stuart was named Duke of Lennox and High Chamberlain in 1581. The title later passed to Charles Lennox, an illegitimate son of Charles II, from whom the Dukes of Richmond and Lennox are descended. Lennox Castle, near Glasgow, was the seat of a cadet branch, Lennox of Woodhead, later recognized as chief of the clan.

LESLIE

Badge: A demi-griffin, with the motto "Grip fast"

Gaelic: *Mac an Fhleisdeir*

The name comes from the estate of Leslie in Aberdeenshire, which was granted by William the Lion to Malcolm, son of a Flemish noble named Bartholf, in the twelfth century. Conversely, Leslie in Fife takes its name from the family who acquired lands there in the thirteenth century. George Leslie was named Earl of Rothes, raised to a dukedom in 1680. John Leslie, Bishop of Ross, was a leading supporter of Mary, Queen of Scots, but the seventeenth century witnessed three Leslies who rose to the highest ranks in the armies of Sweden and the Empire. Alexander Leslie, field marshal under Gustavus Adolphus, became Earl of Leven.

LINDSAY

Badge: A swan rising from a coronet, with the French motto *Endure fort* (Endure bravely)

Gaelic: *MacGhille Fhionnlaigh*

The name originates from Limesay, Norse for "island of lime-trees," a place near Rouen in Normandy. Having come to England with the Conqueror, the first of the family went north, Sir Walter de Lindsay receiving the lands of Ercildoun from David I. His grandson, William, married the daughter of Prince Henry of Scotland and acquired the lands of Crawford in Lanarkshire. David Lindsay married a daughter of Robert II and was named Earl of Crawford in 1398. The clan has a long literary tradition; Sir David Lindsay of the Mount, tutor of James V, wrote *The Three Estaits* (1540) and Robert Lindsay of Pitscottie authored *The Chronicles of Scotland*, while the twenty-sixth earl was a noted bibliophile.

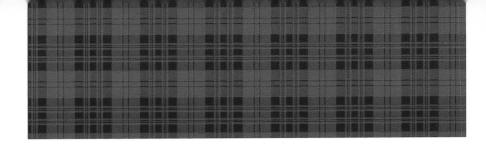

LIVINGSTONE

Badge: A demi-savage, crowned and
wreathed with laurels, holding a club
and a snake, with the French motto
Si je puis (If I can)

Gaelic: *Mac an Leigh*

This is one of the oldest names in Scotland, having been recorded in documents from the eleventh century and derived from the place-name Livingston, in West Lothian. Sir James Livingston of Callendar was raised to the peerage in 1458. William, fifth Lord Livingston, was guardian of the young Mary, Queen of Scots (ruled 1542–67). Alexander, the seventh lord, was named Earl of Linlithgow in 1600 but the title was forfeited when the fifth earl was involved in the 1715 rebellion. The Gaelic name, meaning "son of the physician," alludes to the Livingstones of Argyll, a tradition maintained by their most illustrious descendant, Dr. David Livingstone, known as the missionary-explorer of Africa.

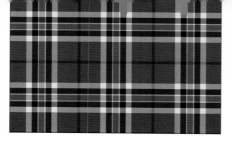

LOCH NESS

LOCKHART

The great tract of water occupying much of the Great Glen is of immense depth and has never been fully surveyed. Tales of monsters inhabiting it have existed since the time of St. Columba in the sixth century and have resulted in a thriving tourist trade. Capitalizing on this, Kiltmakers of Inverness Limited created this trade tartan in 1983, whose somber brown background symbolizes the murky depths of the loch. Since 1934, when a photograph (now proven to have been a fake) appeared to show the monster's head and neck rising out of the water, there have been numerous sightings and almost as many scientific expeditions to track Nessie down. The monster not only has its own tartan but has also been assigned a proper scientific name: *Plesiosaurus rhombopterus nessiterus*, the plesiosaur with rhomboid flippers from Loch Ness.

Badge: A boar's head, with the Latin motto
Corda serrata fero (I bear a locked heart)

This Lowland clan traces its origins back to a Danish adventurer named Lokki or Locard, one of a Viking band, who established an enclave in Dumfriesshire in the eleventh century, and is remembered today in the little town of Lockerbie ("Locard's town"), which was the tragic site of the crash of Pan Am flight 101 in 1988. A later generation of the family acquired the lands of Lee in Lanarkshire. To this day their proudest possession is the celebrated Lee Penny, a charm said to have magic powers, which Sir Simon Lockhart brought back from the Crusades and forms the basis for Sir Walter Scott's historical romance, *The Talisman*. Famous people include John Gibson Lockhart (1794–1854), Scott's son-in-law and biographer.

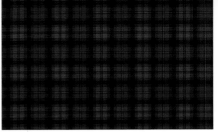

LOGAN

LORNE

Badge: A heart pierced by a nail, with the
    Latin motto *Hoc majorum virtus* (This is
    the valor of my ancestors)
Gaelic: *Loganaich*

The name of this clan derives from a place and a
river (the Logan Water) in Ayrshire, its chiefs being
landowners in the southwest of Scotland by the
twelfth century. Sir Robert Logan and Sir Walter
Logan were named among the followers of the
Black Douglas, killed in Spain in 1329 while taking
the heart of Robert Bruce to the Holy Land. Sir
Robert Logan of Restalrig married a daughter of
Robert II and became Admiral of Scotland. The last
of the line was outlawed and died in his refuge of
Fast Castle, Berwickshire. From the Logans of
Drumderfit come the sept of MacLennan. The most
famous clansman is the comedian Jimmy Logan,
who died in 2002.

Tradition has it that in 498, Fergus MacErch and his
two brothers led a party of Scots who crossed over
from Ireland and settled in Dalriada (modern Argyll).
From Loarn, the younger brother of Fergus, comes
the name of the district called Lorne, lying between
the firth of that name and Loch Fyne on the west
coast of Argyll. It is the heart of the Campbell clan
country and the eldest son of the Duke of Argyll
bears the courtesy title of Marquess of Lorne. In
1871, Princess Louise, fourth daughter of Queen
Victoria, married John Douglas Campbell,
Marquess of Lorne (who became the ninth duke in
1900), and this tartan was created to mark the
event. The sett is based on that of the Campbell
tartan, with the addition of a number of narrow
stripes.

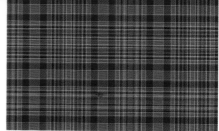

LUMSDEN

Badge: A naked arm and hand brandishing a sword issuing from a coronet, with the Latin motto *Amor patitur moras* (Love endures delays)

In 1098 King Edgar refounded Coldingham Abbey and endowed it with the Berwickshire manor of Lumsden. Easter and Wester Lumsden are recorded in charters between 1166 and 1182. The clan traces its descent from Adam de Lumsden of that ilk in the mid-thirteenth century, and he and his son Roger are listed in the Ragman Rolls of 1296. Thomas Lumsden founded the branch of the clan located at Cushnie in Aberdeenshire in the mid-fifteenth century and from this also come the Lumsdens of Pitcaple in the same county. Sir Harry Lumsden founded Lumsden's Guides, a crack cavalry unit of the Indian Army, and introduced khaki (Urdu for "dust-colored") uniform cloth.

MACALISTER

Badge: A right hand holding a dagger, with the Latin motto *Fortiter* (Boldly)
Gaelic: *MacAlasdair*

The clan traces its origins to Alexander, son of Donald of Islay and great-grandson of Somerled, Lord of the Isles, who acquired lands in Kintyre. By unwisely allying himself with the MacDougalls of Lorne against Robert Bruce, Alexander forfeited his claim to the lordship of the Isles. His descendants expanded out of Knapdale, acquiring other estates in Argyll as well as in Arran and Bute. Alexander MacAlister was an ardent Jacobite who fought at Killiecrankie and the Boyne. The MacAlisters of Tarbert were hereditary constables of Tarbert Castle, Loch Fyne.

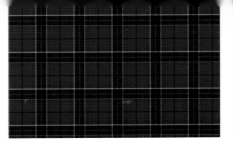 

MACALPINE

Badge: A saracen's head dripping blood,
   with the Gaelic motto *Cuinich bas Alpan*
   (Remember the death of Alpin)
Gaelic: *MacAilpein*

Paradoxically, although this is undoubtedly one of the oldest names in Scotland, the bearers of this surname were generally regarded as septs of the Grants, MacGregors, MacNabs, or MacAulays, the clans belonging to the confederacy known as Siol Alpin (the seed of Alpin). The name goes back to Alpin, King of Scots in the ninth century and father of Kenneth, who became the first King of the Picts and Scots in 843. In more recent times, Robert McAlpine developed one of the country's largest firms of builders and construction engineers and was named baronet in 1918. From him were descended the life peers Baron McAlpine of Moffat and Baron McAlpine of West Green.

MACARTHUR

Badge: A laurel wreath, with the Latin motto
   Fide et opera (By faith and works)
Gaelic: *MacArtair*

"There is nothing older, unless the hills, MacArthur and the devil" is an old Highland saying, testifying to the antiquity of this clan, although it was, in fact, the senior branch of the Campbells. For their support in the War of Independence, Robert Bruce granted the clan estates in Argyll, including those forfeited from the MacDougalls of Lorne, the clan chief being appointed captain of Dunstaffnage Castle near Oban. After the execution of John MacArthur in 1427, the power of the clan waned. The most famous clansmen are John MacArthur, who introduced merino sheep to Australia, and General Douglas MacArthur, both descended from the MacArthurs of Strachur.

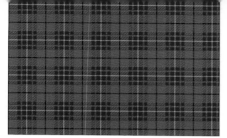

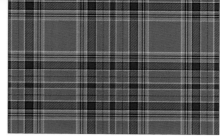

MACAULAY

Badge: An antique boot, with the Latin motto
  Dulce periculum (Peril is sweet)
Gaelic: *MacAmhlaidh*

The name, meaning "son of Olaf," points to a
Norse origin for the MacAulays of Lewis, who claim
descent from Olaf the Black, King of Man and the
Isles in the thirteenth century. Branches of this
family settled in Sutherland and Wester Ross. They
are often regarded as a quite separate clan from
the MacAulays of Dunbartonshire, who were an
offshoot of Siol Alpin (the seed of Alpin). The latter
trace their descent from Aulay, brother of the Earl
of Lennox in the late thirteenth century, who had
his stronghold at Ardincaple near Helensburgh, the
clan seat until 1787 when the twelfth chief sold the
estate to the Duke of Argyll. The historian Lord
MacAulay (1800–59) was a descendant of the
Lewis clan.

MACBEAN

Badge: A demi-cat rampant, with the motto
  "Touch not the cat bot (without) a glove"
Gaelic: *MacBheathain*

As its badge and motto indicate, this clan was a
branch of the Clan Chattan and derives its name
from someone whose epithet means "the fair one,"
as in Donald Ban, King of Scots in the eleventh
century. Claiming descent from MacBeth, the
family hailed from Lochaber but moved to Moray in
the train of a Clan Chattan heiress and settled at
Kinchyle, Strathnairn, and Dores. Gillies MacBean
was one of the heroes of Culloden, killing fourteen
Hanoverian soldiers before he was felled. William
MacBean enlisted in the army, won the Victoria
Cross in the Indian Mutiny, was commissioned, and
rose to the rank of major-general.

 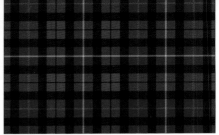

MACBETH

Badge: A mailed arm brandishing a sword
Gaelic: *Mac Bheatha* (Son of life)

This ancient clan derives its name from MacBeth, son of Finnlaec, mormaer (governor) of Moray, whose mother was a daughter of Kenneth II. Born around 1005, he married Gruoch, granddaughter of Kenneth III, which gave him an additional claim to the throne. He killed King Duncan in battle near Elgin in 1040 and usurped the throne, but was in turn killed by Duncan's son, Malcolm Canmore, at the battle of Lumphanan in 1057. Malcolm only won the throne a year later after killing MacBeth's stepson Lulach. Contrary to Shakespeare's version, MacBeth was a wise and devout ruler, who even made a pilgrimage to Rome in 1050. Because of the similarity of names from the same Gaelic root, MacBeth, Bethune, and Beaton are often confused, but variants of MacBeth proper include MacVeigh, Leech, and Leitch.

MACBRIDE

Gaelic: *Mac Gille Brighde* (Son of the servant of St. Bride or Bridget)

St. Bride or Brigid of Kildare (c. 450–523) was one of the most popular Irish saints, much revered in the Highlands and Islands of Scotland, where *gillebrighde* is also the Gaelic name for the oystercatcher. John MacGilbride was the deputy for the Lord of the Isles in Bute, while a person of the same name was Deacon of the Isles a century later. The MacBrides have been followers of the Lords of the Isles and latterly regarded as a sept of the MacDonalds, and the name is widespread in the Hebrides, Argyll, and Ayrshire. Stuart C. MacBride, a member of the Weaver Incorporation of Aberdeen, commissioned Harry Lindley to design a tartan based on the colors in his personal arms. It is a personal tartan, and theoretically anyone wishing to wear it should get permission from the family.

MACCALLUM

Badge: A castle, with the Latin motto
  In ardua tendit (He has attempted
  difficult things)

Gaelic: *MacChaluim*

The name signifies a devotee of St. Columba, the Irish saint who converted the Picts to Christianity in the sixth century, and therefore its history is closely connected to the Clan Malcolm, hence the similarity of the clan badges and mottoes. The MacCallums held lands at Ariskeodnish, Argyll, but acquired estates at Craignish and Lochavich in the fifteenth century. Dugald MacCallum of Poltalloch adopted the surname Malcolm on succeeding to this estate in 1779. The MacCallums were supporters of the Marquess of Argyll in the wars of the seventeenth century, and renowned for their warlike prowess. Famous clansmen include the actors John and David MacCallum.

MACCOLL

Badge: A six-pointed star within the horns of a crescent, with the Latin motto *Justi ut sidera fulgent* (They just shine like stars)

Gaelic: *MacColla*

The name means "son of the high one," and is said to derive from a leading member of the Clan Donald whose lands were at the head of Loch Fyne, bringing them into conflict with the MacGregors and the MacPhersons. At Drum Nachder in 1602, the MacColls were slaughtered by their enemies and thereafter their power and influence in Argyll waned. Famous clansmen include the Gaelic poet Evan MacColl (1808–98), whose monument was unveiled at Kenmore in 1930; R. S. McColl, known as "Toffee Bob" from his confectionery chain; the journalist Ian McColl, a descendant of the McColls of Mull; and the life peer Lord McColl of Dulwich.

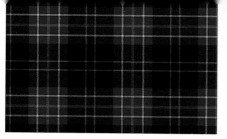

MACDIARMID

Gaelic: *MacDiarmaid*

The name is derived from the Old Irish word *diarmait* (freeman), but first occurs in Scottish records, somewhat phonetically, as MacTarmayt in 1427. By the middle of the fifteenth century it was commonly found in various parts of Lorn and Lochaber, the MacDiarmids being a sept of the Campbells. Alternative spellings are MacDermot and McDermott. The name is also fairly common in Ireland, the most famous clansman being John McDermott (Sean MacDiarmada), one of the leaders of the Easter Rising in 1916 who was executed by the British. Hugh MacDiarmid, Scotland's leading poet in the twentieth century, was actually Christopher Murray Grieve, MacDiarmid being only a pen name.

MACDONALD, FLORA

Badge: A triple-towered castle surmounted by an armored arm holding a sword, with the motto "My hope is constant in thee"
Gaelic: *MacDhomhnuill*

Born near Daliburgh, South Uist, in 1722, Flora MacDonald escorted the fugitive Prince Charles Edward Stuart, disguised as her Irish maid Betty Burke, via Benbecula and "over the sea to Skye" following his defeat at Culloden in 1746. From there he took a ship back to exile in France. Flora was sent to the Tower of London but released in 1747. Three years later she married her kinsman Alan MacDonald of Kingsburgh and emigrated with him to North Carolina. The former Jacobite heroine was now an Empire Loyalist and when her husband was captured by the rebel colonists, she fled to Nova Scotia. When her husband was liberated, they returned to Skye in 1779, where she died at Kilmuir in 1790.

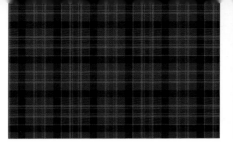

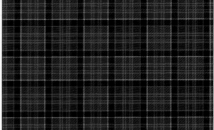

MACDONALD

Badge: Badge: An upright mailed fist holding
a cross-crosslet, with the Latin motto *Per
mare per terras* (By sea and land)
Gaelic: *MacDhomhnuill*

By far the largest and most prolific of all the Scottish
clans, the Clan Donald traces its Pictish and Norse
origins to Donald, grandson of Somerled, King of the
Isles. Somerled had married the daughter of Olaf,
King of Man, and their three sons were founders of
powerful clans such as the MacDougalls of Lorne, as
well as the numerous branches of the MacDonalds.
Clan Donald is now spoken of in terms of its northern
and southern branches, but these have become
separate clans with distinctive tartans and variants on
the original clan emblem. Members include Sir John
MacDonald, Prime Minister of Canada (1867–73 and
1878–91) and Ramsay MacDonald, Prime Minister of
Britain (1924 and 1929–35).

MACDONALD OF CLANRANALD

Badge: A triple-towered castle surmounted
by an armored arm holding a sword, with
the motto "My hope is constant in thee"
Gaelic: *MacDhomhnuill*

The clan takes its name from Reginald or Ranald,
younger son of John, Lord of the Isles, who obtained
lands in the northern Hebrides and mainland in 1373.
The subbranches of the clan are Moidart, Morar,
Knoydart, and Glengarry. A long and bitter feud
between the various factions of the MacDonalds was
only resolved by the showdown known as Blar na
Leine (the field of shirts) in 1544, when MacDonald
fought MacDonald, stripped to the waist. John of
Moidart emerged as the victor. Clanranald supported
the Stewarts in the wars and rebellions of the
seventeenth and eighteenth centuries.

MACDONALD OF GLENCOE

Badge: A phoenix, with the motto "In hope I byde"

Gaelic: *MacDhomhnuill*

This branch of the great Clan Donald regards its progenitor as Iain Abrach, son of Angus Og, and for that reason is sometimes referred to as Maclan. In the aftermath of the Williamite Wars (1689–90), when the Highlands were still unruly, the recalcitrant chiefs were required to take the oath of allegiance by January 1, 1692, or face the consequences. Only one chief was late (purely because he had gone to Fort William to take the oath, but was then redirected to Inveraray) and that was Alexander MacDonald of Glencoe, who had fought at Killiecrankie. His clan was regarded as "a thieving tribe, a damnable sept, the worst in all the Highlands," and the government of William III decided to make an example of them. A party of Campbells, hereditary enemies of the MacDonalds, was sent to Glencoe on February 1 and billeted on the clan. During the night of February 13, they rose up and slew their host and his family. Thirty-eight persons, including several children, were killed, but the others managed to escape into the mountains. There had been worse atrocities in clan feuding, but what makes this particularly despicable was the fact that it was ordered by the government. Ironically, a later MacDonald of Glencoe, Duncan McDonald, married a Nez Perce princess and was an eyewitness to the massacre of his tribe by the U.S. cavalry in August 1877.

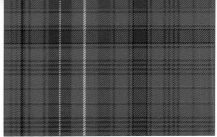

MACDONALD OF SLEAT

Badge: An armored fist holding a cross-crosslet, with the Latin motto *Per mare per terras* (By sea and land)
Gaelic: *MacDhomhnuill*

The MacDonalds of Sleat, Skye, originate from Hugh, third son of Alexander, third Lord of the Isles, who died in 1498. There was a rapid succession of chiefs, either slain in battle or murdered. After centuries of feuding, it was not until 1610 that Donald Gorm Mor, seventh of Sleat, and other island chiefs agreed to keep the king's peace. His nephew and successor, Sir Donald, was named a baronet of Nova Scotia in 1625, but the fourth baronet, known as Sir Donald of the Wars, lost his lands for participating in the 1715 rebellion. Alexander, ninth baronet, was raised to the Irish peerage in 1766 as Baron MacDonald of Slate [*sic*]. Sir Ian Godfrey Bosville MacDonald of Sleat is the seventeenth baronet and twenty-fifth chief.

MACDONALD OF STAFFA

Badge: An upright mailed fist holding a cross-crosslet, with the Latin motto *Per mare per terras* (By sea and land)
Gaelic: *MacDhomhnuill*

This family was originally a cadet branch of the MacDonalds of Clanranald, possessing lands in the Inner Hebrides and taking their name from the small island of Staffa, off the coast of Mull. Uninhabited since the 1850s, Staffa was mainly used for grazing sheep and its beauty was unknown to the outside world until 1772, when a party of scientists led by Sir Joseph Banks stopped off there en route to Iceland and beheld the marvels of Fingal's Cave for the first time. A full description, with an engraving, appeared in Thomas Pennant's book of 1773 and thereafter Staffa was on the tourist trail.

MACDONALD OF THE ISLES

Badge: An upright mailed fist holding a cross-crosslet, with the Latin motto *Per mare per terras* (By sea and land)

Gaelic: *MacDhomhnuill*

Somerled expelled the Norsemen from Arran and Bute in 1135 but fell in battle at Renfrew in 1164 when he challenged Malcolm IV. From his son Reginald (Ranald) came Donald of Islay, progenitor of the clan, whose son, Angus, originally supported Haco of Norway. His son, Angus Og (young Angus) atoned for this by supporting Robert Bruce in the War of Independence, and his son John became Lord of the Isles in 1354. Through marriage, Alexander became Earl of Ross. His son John declared his independence but was defeated by James IV; the title Lord of the Isles was abolished in 1493 and his lands given to the Campbells. John himself died without legitimate issue in 1498.

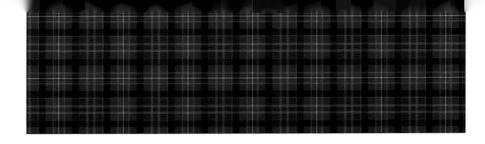

MACDONNELL OF GLENGARRY

Badge: A raven perched on a rock, with
the Gaelic motto *Creagan an fhitich*
(Raven's rock)

Gaelic: *MacDhomhnuill*

This branch of Clan Donald is descended from Donald, eldest son of Ranald, and is a branch of Clanranald. The distinctive spelling of the surname was adopted in the seventeenth century. From Alasdair, fourth chief of Glengarry, the clan takes its Gaelic patronymic of Mac 'ic Alasdair. Eneas of Glengarry was one of the earliest supporters of Montrose, forfeited by Cromwell in 1651 but named Lord MacDonell at the Restoration. The clan members were ardent Jacobites who fought at Killiecrankie and in the rebellions of 1715 and 1745–46. A famous clansman was James McDonnell, the American aircraft pioneer.

MACDONNELL OF KEPPOCH

Badge: A triple-towered castle surmounted
by an armored arm holding a sword, with
the motto "My hope is constant in thee"

Gaelic: *MacDhomhnuill*

Originally a branch of the Clanranald MacDonalds based in Lochaber, this clan traces its origins from Alasdair Carrach, third son of John, first Lord of the Isles, and a grandson of Robert II. There was a long-running feud between this clan and the Mackintoshes, largely because the MacDonnells occupied their land by custom, in defiance of a charter that had been granted to the Mackintoshes. Matters came to a head at Blar na Leine in 1544, for his part in which Ranald MacDonnell was executed. Successive chiefs were outlawed, but gained distinction in the armies of Sweden and Spain. The Well of the Heads in Invergarry commemorates the beheading of the seven men who murdered the twelfth chief in 1663. The clan struck the first blow in the "Forty-five," capturing government troops at Glenfinnan before the rebellion commenced.

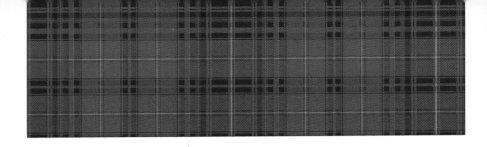

MACDOUGALL

Badge: A bent right arm in armor, holding a
cross-crosslet, with the Latin motto
Vincere et mori (To win or die)

Gaelic: *MacDhugaill*

The clan takes its name from Dougal, son of Somerled of the Isles. Dougal's son Duncan received lands in Lorne and his son, Ewin, married a daughter of the Red Comyn murdered by Robert Bruce at Dumfries in 1306. As a result, the MacDougalls were sworn enemies of the Bruce, who, fleeing from his enemies, discarded his cloak and a large brooch, ever afterward known as the Brooch of Lorne and an important clan treasure. Years later, a granddaughter of Bruce married the chief but their son John died without issue and his lands passed to the Stewarts of Lorne in 1388. The chiefship later passed to John MacAlan MacDougall of Dunollie. Iain Ciar was forfeited in 1715, but the clan lands were restored in 1745 when it remained loyal to the Hanoverian cause.

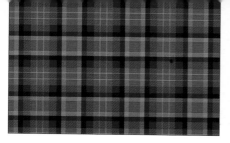

MACDUFF

Badge: A demi-lion rampant holding a
   dagger, with the Latin motto *Deus juvat*
   (God helps)
Gaelic: *MacDhuibh*

MacDuff (son of the dark man) was a patronymic of
the Celtic Earls of Fife, the first of whom overthrew
MacBeth in 1056 and helped Malcolm Canmore
regain the throne. Succeeding generations had the
role of crowning the king. Duncan, Earl of Fife, having
allied himself to Edward I, refused to crown Robert
Bruce, but his sister Isabel, Countess of Buchan,
performed this duty instead. The earldom died out in
1353 but was revived in the eighteenth century.
Alexander Duff (1849–1912), Earl of MacDuff and
Duke of Fife, founded the British South Africa
Company. His wife was Princess Louise, daughter of
Edward VII, and their daughter, Princess Alexandra
Victoria, married Prince Arthur, Duke of Connaught.

MACEWEN

Badge: The stump of an oak tree sprouting
   young branches, with the Latin motto
   Reviresco (I grow green)
Gaelic: *MacEoghainn*

According to the historian Skene, this clan, with the
MacNeills and MacLachlans, formed the Siol
Gillivray (the seed of Gillivray) and was in existence
long before 1450, holding lands at Otter on the
shores of Loch Fyne, where the ancient ruins of
MacEwen's Castle can be seen to this day. The
progenitor of this clan flourished at the beginning of
the thirteenth century, but Swene MacEwen, ninth
and last chief, surrendered his lands to Duncan
Campbell in 1432. This landless clan was then
scattered all over the Highlands and the southwest
of Scotland.

MACFADYEN

Badge: No known badge

Gaelic: *MacPhaidein*

The name means "son of little Patrick," and is of Irish origin, the earliest record being of a Padyne Regan living in Dublin in 1264. People of this name were settled in Mull by the beginning of the fourteenth century and among the various spellings recorded thereafter are MacFadyen, MacFadyean, and MacFadzean—the latter probably the most common form today. The MacFaddens were originally a sept of the MacLeans or MacLaines. Famous clansmen include Sir Frank (later Lord) MacFadzean; Lord MacFadyen, a Scottish lawlord; and Jean MacFadden, one of Glasgow's most prominent political figures for the last thirty years.

MACFARLANE

Badge: A demi-savage holding a sheaf of arrows and an imperial crown, with the motto "This I'll defend"

Gaelic: *MacPharlain*

This clan from Loch Lomondside is descended from Gilchrist, brother of the third Earl of Lennox in the thirteenth century. Gilchrist's great-grandson was Bartholomew, rendered in Gaelic as "Parlan." Duncan, the sixth chief, obtained the estate of Arrochar from the Earl of Lennox in 1395. Intermarriage with the Lennox family brought the MacFarlanes close to the crown in the sixteenth century, but at Langside (1567) they were prominent in their opposition to Mary, Queen of Scots. Backing the wrong side in the conflicts of the seventeenth century, the clan was outlawed and many emigrated to Ireland and America (where the present chief resides).

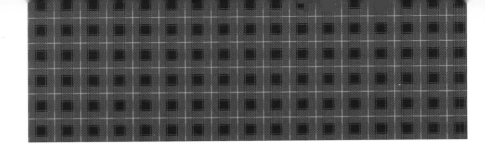

MACFIE or MACPHEE

Badge: A demi-lion rampant, with the Latin
motto *Pro rege* (For the king)

Gaelic: *MacDubh-shithe*

The Gaelic name translates as "dark of peace" and is sometimes rendered phonetically as MacCuish or MacDuffie. Dubhshith was a reader at Iona in 1164, but the origins of this clan are lost in the mists of antiquity; it claimed to belong to Siol Alpin (the seed of Alpin). This clan had the distinction of possessing the island of Colonsay, with a burial ground on the tidal islet of Oronsay, but the island passed from their hands in the mid-seventeenth century. As a landless clan, the MacPhees were scattered all over Scotland, giving rise to such variants as Cathie, Fee, MacGuffie, and MacHaffie. Ewen MacPhee earned notoriety in the nineteenth century as "the last Scottish outlaw." Having deserted from the army, he squatted on an island in Loch Quoich, but in old age was evicted for stealing sheep.

MACGILL

Gaelic: *Mac an Ghoill* (Son of the stranger)

The name of this clan implies that its progenitor was an incomer, i.e., a person who had migrated from the Lowlands and settled in Galloway, which remained Celtic and Gaelic-speaking long after the rest of southern Scotland had become anglicized. The surname, sometimes spelled MakGill, is still very common in Galloway. A branch of this clan subsequently settled in Jura, where it was known as Clann a' ghoill (children of the stranger). The name is an ancient one, recorded in documents from 1231 onward. From the Wigtownshire branch came the Reverend William McGill (1752–1807), a highly controversial theologian. James McGill (1744–1813) amassed a fortune in Canada and founded the Montreal university that bears his name. Another famous person of this name was Donald McGill, the prolific artist of saucy seaside postcards, actually the pseudonym of Fraser Gould (1875–1962).

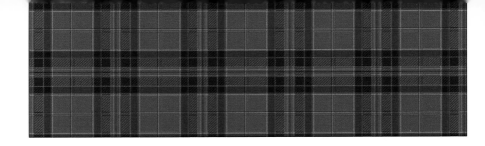

MACGILLIVRAY

Badge: A seated cat, with the motto "Touch not the cat bot (without) a glove"

Gaelic: *MacGhille-brath*

The Gaelic name, which translates as "son of the servant of judgment," points to an hereditary judgeship enjoyed by the clan's progenitor, but nothing is known for certainty beyond the fact that it belonged to Clan Chattan and was formerly very numerous in Morven, Lochaber, and Mull. In one of the many upheavals of the late Middle Ages, however, the clan was displaced by one of the royal expeditions against the Highlands and Islands and placed itself under the protection of the Mackintoshes, obtaining lands in Strathnairn. At Culloden, Alexander MacGillivray of Dunmaglas led Clan Chattan to victory over the left wing of the Hanoverian army.

MACGREGOR

Badge: A crowned lion's head, with the
  Gaelic motto *Is rioghail mo dhream*
  (Royal is my race)

Gaelic: *MacGrioghair*

The motto alludes to the claim that the clan is descended from Greg MacGraith, an eighth-century King of the Picts, recalled in the place-names Ecclesgreig and St. Cyrus in Kincardineshire. The earliest references to the clan, however, place it in Glenorchy in the twelfth century. Warlike and unruly, they were harassed and persecuted by their neighbors, and finally proscribed in 1603. This was revoked by Charles II but reapplied by William III and it was not until 1775 that the MacGregors were amnestied. The most famous clansmen are Rob Roy MacGregor (1671–1743) and the Norwegian composer Edvard Grieg, whose Scottish grandfather settled in Bergen.

MACGREGOR OF GLENSTRAE

Badge: A crowned lion's head, with the
   Gaelic motto *Is rioghail mo dhream*
   (Royal is my race)
Gaelic: *MacGrioghair*

Although the Clan Gregor originated in Glenorchy, important branches settled in adjoining valleys in the mountainous region that separates Perthshire from Argyll. Thus arose the major branches of the MacGregors of Glengyle, Glenlochy, and Glenstrae, whose chiefs were the sons of One-eyed Iain (died 1390). The most notorious of the clan was, of course, Rob Roy, who was the third son of Donald Glas (died 1702), the fifth chief of Glengyle. The Glenstrae branch of the clan was descended from One-eyed Iain's second son, Iain Dhubh. A daughter of this clan married a Campbell and this gave rise to that clan's ambitions to take over all the territory of Clan Gregor, which they did so ruthlessly and efficiently that the landless MacGregors came to be known as the Children of the Mist.

MACHARDY

Gaelic: *Mac Chardaidh* (Son of the sloe)

This small family held lands in Strathdon and Braemar from the fifteenth century and attached itself to the more powerful clans of the area. The Strathdon branch allied themselves to the Mackintoshes and became a member of the confederation of Clan Chattan. In the Braemar district, however, they were regarded as a sept of the Farquharsons of Invercauld. A Thomas McChardy was arraigned for murder in 1560, while such variants as McQuardies, McKardie, and McArdie appear in various seventeenth-century records from Aberdeenshire. As well as the variant MacHardie, it should be noted that members of the clan migrating to the Lowlands or England often dropped the "Mac" prefix. Famous persons of this name include the pioneer socialist Keir Hardie (1856–1915), the novelist Thomas Hardy (1840–1928), and Nelson's flag captain at Trafalgar, later Admiral Sir Thomas Hardy (1769–1839).

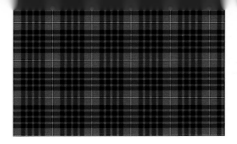

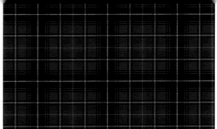

MACIAN

Badge: A phoenix, with the motto "In hope
I byde"
Gaelic: *Mac Iain* (Son of John)

This surname was borne by several branches
of Clan Donald. As well as the MacDonalds
of Glencoe, there were the MacIans of
Ardnamurchan, who traced their descent from a
son of Angus Mór, Lord of the Isles, Eoin
Sprangach (John of the four-pronged hay fork),
who flourished in the most westerly district of the
Scottish mainland in the fourteenth century. A
branch of this family migrated to Elgin in the
seventeenth century and adopted the spelling
MacKeane. Variant spellings of this surname
include MacKean, McKeen, Keen(e), Caine, and
MacKain.

MACINNES

Badge: A bee sucking a thistle, with the Latin
motto *E labore dulcedo* (Pleasure comes
from work)
Gaelic: *MacAonghais*

This clan claims to be one of the oldest, although
its connection with the Cineal Angus, one of the
three tribes of Dalriada in the fifth century, seems
doubtful, as the clan had no lands in that district.
They first appear in recorded history in the twelfth
century, residing in Morven, where they were
constables of Kinlochaline Castle, overlooking the
Sound of Mull, until 1645. The MacInneses were
also hereditary archers to Clan MacKinnon, hence
the branch of the clan that settled in Skye.

MACINROY

Gaelic: *Mac Iain Ruaidh* (Son of Red John)

The progenitor of this Perthshire clan was Red John of Straloch, connected to the Reids and Robertsons of Atholl. The earliest record of a person of this surname occurs in a charter of Straloch, dated 1539. Thereafter, there are numerous references to MacInroys in and around Pitlochry. Most famous of the clan was James MacInroy of Lude (1759–1825), known locally as "the pirate" on account of the fortune he accumulated as a privateer in the West Indies during the French Revolutionary and Napoleonic Wars. The celebrated poet, Madeline MacInroy (1862–1925), was his great-granddaughter. Variants of the name include McEnroe, the most famous of whom is the tennis player, John McEnroe.

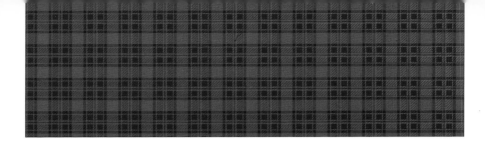

MACINTOSH or MACKINTOSH

Badge: A cat salient, with the motto "Touch not the cat bot (without) a glove"

Gaelic: *Mac an Toisich* (Son of the thane)

The Gaelic name denotes a descent from the senior cadet of a clan, and the Mackintoshes have, indeed, been regarded as one of the most prominent branches of the Clan Chattan for a long time—as a result of the marriage in 1291 of Angus, sixth of MacIntosh, to Eva, the heiress of Clan Chattan. The rise of this powerful clan, however, was resented by the Earls of Moray and Huntly, as well as neighboring clans. Mackintosh chiefs had a rather quirky record, one leading the Covenanters of the North, but another opposing Cromwell, and a third supporting William of Orange. Yet the clan is best remembered for its role in the later Jacobite rebellions. Brigadier MacIntosh of Borlum was a Jacobite general in 1715. Thirty years later, Mackintosh of Mackintosh served in the Hanoverian army while his wife raised the clan that routed the government forces at Moy.

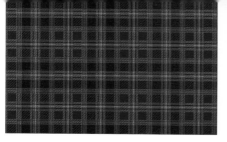

MACINTYRE

Badge: A right hand holding a dagger, with
the Latin motto *Per ardua* (Through
struggles)

Gaelic: *Mac an t-Saoir*

The name translates as "son of the carpenter,"
hence the name Wright, which is a sept of the clan,
along with MacTear and MacTire. It seems probable
that this large clan arose from the profession of
carpentry, rather than the fanciful explanation that it
once held lands in Kintyre, and this explains why it
was so widespread all over the Highlands. The chief
family held lands in Glencoe until 1806 when the
lands were sold, and many clansmen migrated to
America. Various branches of the clan held office as
hereditary foresters to the Stewarts of Appin, or
pipers to Clanranald, and Clan Menzies. The most
famous clansman is Duncan MacIntyre, the
celebrated Gaelic poet (1724–1812).

MACIVER

Badge: A boar's head, with the Latin motto
Nunquam obliviscar (I shall never forget)

Gaelic: *Mac Iomhair*

Tradition claims that this clan formed part of the
expedition of Alexander II, which subjugated Argyll
in 1221 and received the lands of Glassary as a
reward. From there they expanded into Cowal and
Lochaber, although later branches also settled in
Glenelg. By the sixteenth century the clan had
broken up and many clansmen then assumed the
name of Campbell, although the name MacIver
survived on the isle of Lewis and in the westerly
parts of Ross-shire.

MACKAY

Badge: A hand holding a dagger, with the
Latin motto *Manu forti* (With a strong hand)

Gaelic: *MacAoidh*

Known also as Clan Morgan from Morgan, son of Magnus in the early fourteenth century, the clan traces its descent from Morgan's grandson Aodh (Hugh), whose mother was a MacNeil of Gigha. This large and powerful clan occupied lands in the far northwest of Scotland and was frequently at odds with its neighbors, the Earls of Caithness and Sutherland. Noted for their warlike spirit, they were recruited by Sir Donald Mackay of Farr to serve under Gustavus Adolphus in the Thirty Years' War (1618–48). Sir Donald was raised to the peerage in 1628 as Lord Reay. His grandson Aeneas commanded the Mackay regiment of the Dutch army and his family was ennobled by William V of Orange. Baron Eric Mackay van Ophemert became the twelfth Lord Reay and clan chief, and his son, the thirteenth Lord Reay, became a naturalized British subject in 1938.

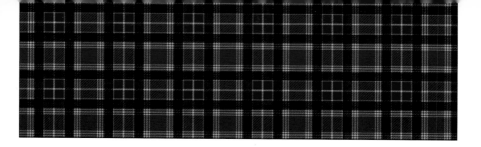

MACKELLAR

Badge: A boar's head, with the Latin motto *Ne obliviscaris* (Do not forget)

Gaelic: *Mac Ealair* (Son of Hilary)

The origin of the Gaelic name is a curious one. It comes from St. Hilarius (c. 315–368), which also created the Hilary term in British courts. It seems more probable that the clan derives its name more immediately from Hilaire, Bishop of Poitiers around 1230, and this points to a French or Norman connection. Be that as it may, the family was well-established in Argyll by the fourteenth century, where it was regarded as a sept of the Campbells. A branch of the family settled in Dumfriesshire, where they dropped the "Mac" prefix. The most well-known member of this clan is the singer Kenneth MacKellar.

MACKENZIE

Badge: An inflamed mountain, with the Latin
motto *Luceo non uro* (I shine, not burn)

Gaelic: *MacCoinnich*

This clan is descended from Kenneth, son of Colin of the Aird, who was first Earl of Ross in the late thirteenth century. Murdoch, son of Kenneth, was granted Kintail in Wester Ross by David II in 1362. Intermarriage with MacDonalds linked the MacKenzies to the Lords of the Isles, but they later became deadly enemies and in 1491 the MacKenzies slaughtered the MacDonalds at Blair na Park. Support for the crown was rewarded by land, and by 1609, when Kenneth became Lord MacKenzie, the clan possessed all the territory from Ardnamurchan to Strathnaver. Colin, second Lord, became Earl of Seaforth in 1623. Forfeited for participation in the "Forty-five," the chief was restored in 1788 after raising the Seaforth Highlanders.

MACKINLAY

Gaelic: *Mac Fhionnlaigh* (Son of Finlay)

Opinion is divided regarding the origin of this surname. Some maintain that it is derived from Fionnlaigh Mór, who bore the royal standard at the Battle of Pinkie in 1547, and this accords with the origins of the Finlaysons of Lochalsh, Dunblane, and Aberdeenshire, who are regarded as septs of the Farquharsons of Braemar. The alternative version is that the progenitor of the family was Finlay, son of Buchanan of Drumkill, near Kilmarnock. From this branch came John MacKinlay (1819–72), the Australian explorer, whereas William McKinley (1843–1901), the U.S. president, was descended from a branch of the Perthshire Finlaysons. Other variants of the name include Finlay, Findlay, Finley, and McGinley. The German scientists Herbert and Erwin Finlay-Freundlich were descended through their mother from the Finlaysons of Dunblane.

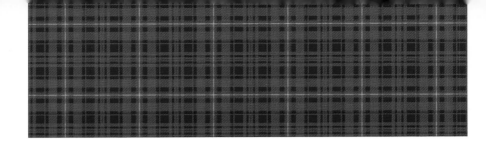

MACKINNON

Badge: A boar's head with a deer's
shankbone in its mouth, with the Latin
motto *Audentes fortuna juvat* (Fortune
helps the daring)

Gaelic: *MacFhionghuin*

The clan claims descent from Fingon, great-grandson of Kenneth MacAlpin, but the earliest records show them in Mull as dependents of the Lord of the Isles, and the last abbot of Iona at the Reformation was John MacKinnon. The clan supported Montrose at Inverlochy (1645) and took part in the Jacobite rebellions, for which the estates were forfeited. The chiefship then passed in 1808 to a descendant of Donald MacKinnon, who had emigrated to Antigua.

MACKIRDY

Gaelic: *Mac Mhuircherach* (Son of the
sea king)

The origin of this surname points to a maritime ancestor and this accords with the fact that people with the name MacKirdy or MacCurdy are still most commonly found in the islands of Arran and Bute, where they were traditionally regarded as a sept of the Stuarts of Bute. The suggestion that the name is derived from a Viking marauder named Myrkjartan, referred to in the Icelandic sagas, is not implausible. Phonetic renderings of the name as Makwrerdy and Makwrarty, both recorded in documents of 1506, provide a clue to the former theory as the likeliest source of the name. Most famous of this name was Douglas McCurdy, whose Canadian biplane, *Silver Dart* (1911), was the first aircraft built in the British Empire.

MACLACHLAN

Badge: A triple-towered castle, with the Latin motto *Fortis et fides* (Brave and trusty)

Gaelic: *MacLachlainn*

This clan was domiciled in Strathlachlan from early times, claiming descent from the ancient kings of Ireland. Documents from 1230 onward testify to successive chiefs, and in 1298 Gilleskel MacLachlan received a charter from John Baliol. The clan fought under Argyll and later Bonnie Dundee at Killiecrankie. The clan chief, serving as aide to Prince Charles, was killed at Culloden. The estates were forfeited, but his son Robert obtained them again in 1749. Branches of the clan are also located in Lochaber, Perthshire, and Stirlingshire.

MACLAINE OF LOCHBUIE

Badge: A battle-ax flanked by branches of
laurel and cypress, with the Latin motto
Vincere vel mori (To conquer or die)

Gaelic: *Mac Ghilleathan* (Son of Gillean)

This ancient clan traces its origin to Gilleathan na Tuaidh (Gillean of the Battle-ax), hence the clan badge. Gillean and his three sons claimed descent from the sixth-century kings of Dalriada and fought valiantly at Largs in 1263. As a result, they were rewarded by Alexander III with lands in southeast Mull and founded the Clan MacLean. This divided in the fourteenth century following a dispute over the chiefship, the Lochbuie branch siding with Eachan Reaganach (Hector the Stern), who opposed Lachlan Lubanach, the head of the MacLeans of Duart. Hector built his stronghold at Lochbuie around 1350 and did homage to the Lord of the Isles. John Mór, the seventh chief, was a renowned swordsman and it was his son Hector who anglicized the surname and adopted the spelling MacLaine. Murdoch, twenty-third of MacLaine, had a very distinguished military career and was decorated with the Iron Cross by Kaiser Wilhelm I. Famous members include actress Shirley MacLaine, though her real name is Shirley MacLean Beaty.

MACLAREN

Badge: The Virgin Mary and infant Jesus, with the Gaelic motto *Bi 'se Mac-an-t-slaurie* (Be thou the son of the crook)

Gaelic: *MacLabhruinn.*

Various accounts traced this clan back to Lorn, son of Erc, who came to Argyll in 503, or St. Lawrence, or three brothers who supported Kenneth MacAlpin, from whom they obtained the lands of Balquhidder and Strathearn. The clan fought for the crown at Sauchieburn (1488), Flodden (1513), and Pinkie (1547); at other times they waged war on their neighbors. The clan was decimated at Culloden. The chiefship was long in abeyance until John McLaurin, Lord Dreghorn, successfully petitioned for the title on grounds of descent from the MacLarens of Tiree.

MACLAY

Gaelic: *Mac Dhuinn-shléibhe* (Son of Donlevy)

This clan, with the surnames MacLay, MacLeay, McCloy, or McDonlevy, was traditionally regarded as a sept of the Stewarts of Appin or the Buchanans of Lennox, tracing their origins back to one Donlevy or Dunsleve (both anglicized versions of a Gaelic name literally meaning "of the brown hill"). The earliest recorded version of the name pertains to James Mac Dunsleph, who was a follower of Robert the Bruce in the early fourteenth century, while Duncan McDunlewe was parish minister of Kilmarnock in 1541. The MacLeays of Lismore were hereditary keepers of the crozier of St. Moluag. This branch of the clan migrated to the mainland, where they anglicized their name as Livingstone. Members of this clan include the American jurist John Jay McCloy (1895–1989), the statesman and signatory of the Declaration of Independence Robert Livingston (1746–1813), and the missionary explorer David Livingstone (1813–73).

MACLEAN

Badge: A battlemented tower, with the motto
"Virtue mine honor"

Gaelic: *MacGhille Eoin*

Despite the Gaelic name meaning "son of the follower of St. John," the clan claims descent from Gilleathain na Tuaidh (Gillian of the Battle-ax) in the thirteenth century. From him were descended the brothers Lachlan Lubanach and Eachan Reaganach, respective founders of the MacLeans of Duart and the MacLaines of Lochbuie in Mull. The clan fought at Harlaw (1411), Flodden (1513), Inverlochy (1645), Killiecrankie (1689), and Culloden, where seven brothers gave their lives to protect the clan chief, to no avail.

MACLEOD OF HARRIS

Badge: A bull's head between two flags, with the Latin motto *Muros aheneus esto* (Be then a wall of brass)

Gaelic: *MacLeoid*

Leod, son of Olaf the Black, derived his name from the Norse word *ljot* (ugly). From his sons Tormod and Torquil came the two main branches of the clan, respectively the MacLeods of Glenelg, Harris, and Dunvegan, and the MacLeods of Lewis, Waternish, and Assynt. Support for the crown gave Siol Tormod (the seed of Tormod) the lands of Glenelg (1343) and northwestern Skye (1498). The clan was almost wiped out at the battle of Worcester (1651), which explains why the clan was absent from the later Jacobite rebellions.

MACLEOD OF LEWIS

Badge: A radiate sun, with the Latin motto
Luceo non uro (I shine, not burn)

Gaelic: *MacLeoid*

This clan held lands in Lewis under the Lords of the Isles, but in the fourteenth century David II gave Torquil MacLeod the barony of Assynt on the mainland, and over the years added estates in Gairloch, Raasay, and Waternish. The history of this clan is one of interminable feuds, not only with other clans but also with the MacLeods of Harris.

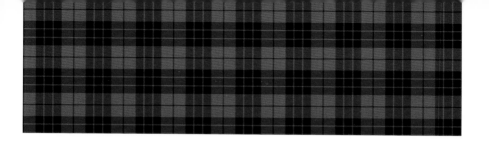

MACLEOD OF RAASAY

Badge: A bull's head between pennants, with the Latin motto *Luceo non uro* (I shine, not burn)

Gaelic: *MacLeoid*

This branch of the Clan MacLeod was descended from Siol Torcuil or the MacLeods of Lewis, through Rough Malcolm, younger brother of Ruaridh MacLeod, tenth chief of the MacLeods of Lewis, who acquired the barony of Assynt in Wester Ross. With the death of Torquil MacLeod of Lewis in 1597, the barony passed to MacKenzie of Coigeach, who had married Torquil's daughter Margaret. As a result, the chiefship devolved on the MacLeods of Raasay, the island that lies between the east coast of Skye and the mainland of Ross-shire. In the eighteenth century the Laird of Raasay built a fine mansion, where Johnson and Boswell stayed during their Highland tour in 1773. His son John and daughter Isabella were close friends of the poet Robert Burns.

MACLINTOCK

Motto: *Virtute et labore* (By valor and hard work)

Gaelic: *Mac Gille-Fhionndaig* (Son of the servant of St. Findon)

As the Gaelic name suggests, this clan probably originated from followers or devotees of St. Findon (Finnan or Fintan), but as there are several Celtic saints of those names, it is impossible to be more precise. Tradition, however, assigns this role to Fintan Munnu, a disciple of Columba who died around 635. At any rate, this surname was prevalent on Loch Lomond-side and Argyll from about 1500 and is regarded as a sept of the MacDougalls of Lorne. *The Book of the Dean of Lismore* includes verses ascribed to a McGillindak. The most famous member of this clan was the industrialist Sir William McLintock (1873–1937).

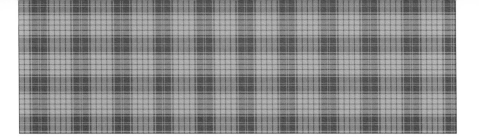

MACMILLAN

Badge: Hands brandishing a two-handed sword, with the Latin motto *Miseris succerere disco* (I learn to succor the unfortunate)

Gaelic: *MacGhilleMhaolain*

The name translates as "son of the servant of the tonsured one," indicating monastic origins. The clan resided in the lands around Loch Arkaig by the twelfth century but then transplanted to Tayside. Later expelled, one branch moved to Knapdale and the other to Galloway, where they became staunch Covenanters. Daniel MacMillan, the Arran crofter who founded the great London publishing house, was the grandfather of Prime Minister Harold MacMillan (1957–63).

MACNAB

Badge: A savage's head, with the Latin
motto *Timor omnis abesto* (Let fear be
far from all)

Gaelic: *Mac an Aba*

The name means "son of the abbot" and, like MacMillan, points to ecclesiastical origins, the clan claiming descent from the hereditary abbots of Glendochart. This once-powerful clan backed the MacDougalls in their feud with the Bruce and suffered as a consequence, as they were deprived of most of their lands after Bannockburn. Their fortunes recovered in later centuries, supporting the Stewarts in the civil wars of the seventeenth century. Although the clan supported Prince Charles in 1745, the chief sided with the Hanoverians and kept his lands intact.

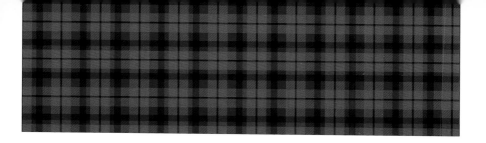

MACNAUGHTON

Badge: An embattled castle, with the motto "I hope in God"

Gaelic: *MacNeachdainn*

The name means "son of the pure one," allegedly Nachtan Mor in the tenth century. This ancient Celtic clan was one of those transplanted from Moray after the uprising of the twelfth century, and resettled in Strathtay. From there they gradually expanded, acquiring lands on the shores of Loch Awe and Loch Fyne. The main line became extinct and the estates disposed of in 1691, and it was not until 1878 that the clan elected a new chief, Sir Alexander MacNaughtan of Bushmills, Ireland, a direct descendant of Shane Dubh, who migrated in 1580.

MACNEILL

Badge: A rock, with the Latin motto *Vincere vel mori* (Conquer or die)

Gaelic: *MacNeill*

Neil Og (young Nigel) received lands in Kintyre from Robert Bruce, and from this root came the two main branches of the clan associated with Barra and Gigha. They respectively allied themselves with the MacLeans of Duart and the Lords of the Isles. As islanders, the MacNeills were noted seafarers, a tradition maintained by the MacNeill who designed the *Queen Mary* and the *Queen Elizabeth*. General Roderick MacNeill was forced to sell Barra in 1863, but in the mid-twentieth century the American architect Robert Lister MacNeil purchased Kisimul Castle and restored it. His son, a professor of law at Cornell University, is the present chief.

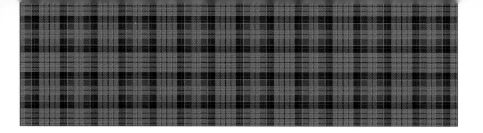

MACNICOL

Badge: A demi-lion rampant, with the Latin motto *Generositate* (With generosity)

Gaelic: *MacNeacail*

The MacNicols or Nicolsons held lands in Coigach and Assynt granted by the Thane of Sutherland, but when Assynt passed by marriage of the MacNicol heiress to the MacLeods, the MacNicols moved to Skye, settling at Scorrybreck. Thereafter, the name of Nicolson features frequently in the history of that island as well as Lewis. The most famous clansman was John Nicholson (1822–57), veteran of many Indian campaigns.

MACPHAIL

Gaelic: *Mac Phàil* (Son of Paul)

As this surname is formed from a very popular forename, it is quite widespread throughout Scotland, especially in the far northwest, and is regarded as a sept of the Mackays. This particular clan traces its origins back to Paul, son of Neil Mackay, and in a rent-roll of the Reay (Mackay) estates in 1678, the surname is very abundant. Others regard themselves as septs of Clan Cameron, the Mackintoshes, or Clan Chattan.

Variants of the name include MacVail and MacFaul as well as Paul, Paulson, Polson, Pawson, and Nelson. Most famous of the clan was James MacPhail, who migrated to England in 1785 and pioneered new methods of raising vegetables. Agnes MacPhail (1890–1954) was Canada's first female member of parliament (1921–40) and also represented her country in the League of Nations.

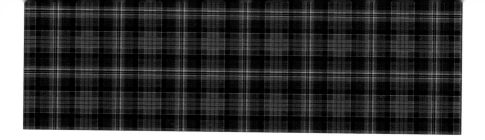

MACPHERSON

Badge: A seated cat, with the motto "Touch not the cat bot (without) a glove"

Gaelic: *Mac a' Phearsoin*

This powerful branch of Clan Chattan traces its descent from Murdoch, the Parson of Kingussie (hence the alternative Gaelic name of MacMhuirich), the family of Cluny emerging as the chief by the late sixteenth century. Involvement in the Jacobite rebellions resulted in forfeiture and exile, but the estates were restored to Duncan MacPherson in 1784 for services rendered in the American Revolutionary War.

MACQUARRIE

Badge: A mailed arm emerging from a crown and holding a dagger, with the Latin motto *Turris fortis mihi Deus* (God is a strong tower to me)

Gaelic: *MacGuaidhre*

The name means "son of the proud man," but is a Gaelic rendering of the Norman "Godfrey." The clan claims descent from Siol Alpin (the seed of Alpin) through a brother of Fingon, and occupied the western part of Mull and the island of Ulva. Lachlan, sixteenth of Ulva, entertained Johnson and Boswell on their tour of the Hebrides but was forced to sell his estates in 1778. Last chief of the MacQuarries, he lived to the age of 103. The most famous clansman is Sir Lachlan MacQuarrie, Governor of New South Wales and founder of Sydney.

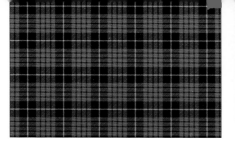

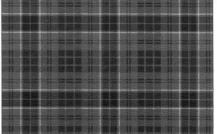

MACQUEEN

Badge: A wolf rampant holding an arrow,
   with the motto "Constant and faithful"
Gaelic: *MacShuibhne*

The name means "son of the good going," but
points to a Norse origin and a progenitor named
Sweyn. The castle and loch called Sween in Argyll
are reminders of the ancient clan lands, although
MacQueens were also to be found in Skye, Lewis,
and even St. Kilda. The chief branch moved to
Strathdearn in Moray and allied themselves to the
MacKintoshes. Famous clansmen include Robert
MacQueen, the infamous judge Lord Braxfield, and
Finlay MacQueen, last of the St. Kilda cragsmen.

MACRAE

Badge: A hand grasping a sword, with the
   Latin motto *Fortitudine* (With fortitude)
Gaelic: *MacRath* (Son of grace)

The name has been traced back to a family living in
the Beauly area in the twelfth century, transplanted
to Kintail in Wester Ross in the fourteenth century,
where Fionnla Dubh had his seat at Eilean Donan.
Although the MacRaes were heavily involved in the
civil wars of the seventeenth century and fought
heroically at Sheriffmuir (1715), they were not
involved in later Jacobite rebellions. Ironically, their
stronghold was destroyed after it was occupied by
Spanish troops in the rebellion of 1719, but was
restored in the twentieth century.

MACTAGGART

Badge: A masonic tower, with the motto "For Commonwealth and Liberty"

Gaelic: *Mac an-t-Sagairt* (Son of the priest)

At first glance it would appear that some priest broke his vows of celibacy, but the first person of this name was Ferquhard MacIntaggart, known as the "son of the red priest of Applecross," actually a lay abbot noted for his forceful Christianity. In 1215 he suppressed an uprising, beheaded the ringleaders, and sent their heads to Alexander II, who knighted him and later conferred on him the earldom of Ross. For this reason the MacTaggarts are regarded as a sept of Clan Ross. Families of this surname also occur in Dumfriesshire but may be unconnected with the Ross-shire clan. One of the Dumfries family, Catherine McTarget, was accused of witchcraft in 1688. Famous persons of this name include the landscape painter William McTaggart (1835–1910); his grandson Sir William MacTaggart (1903–81), president of the Royal Scottish Academy; and David McTaggart, the Canadian-born founder of Greenpeace International. The crest is that of Sir John MacTaggart and alludes to the well-known construction company founded by his grandfather.

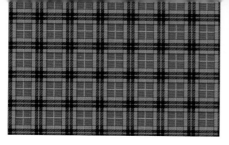

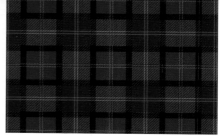

MACTAVISH

Motto: *Non oblitus* (Not forgotten)
Gaelic: *Mac Thamhais* (Son of Tammas)

Tammas was, at one time, a common Lowland form of "Thomas," and it is most unusual for a Gaelic name to be formed from a Lowland Scots word. The progenitor of this clan was Tavis Corr, the natural son of Gillespick of Dunardarie, who possessed these lands of the Earls of Argyll from the fourteenth century. This was confirmed by a charter of 1533 and remained in the possession of the clan chief until 1785. As such, the clan is usually regarded as a sept of the Campbells, although a branch of the family in Stratherrick, Inverness-shire, was associated with Clan Fraser. Members of the Stratherrick family prospered in Canada, especially Simon McTavish (1750–1804), chairman of the North-West Company, who purchased the Dunardarie estate in 1799.

MACTHOMAS

Badge: A wildcat wrestling with a snake, with the Latin motto *Deo juvante invidiam superabo* (With God's help I will rise above envy)
Gaelic: *Mac Thómais* (Son of Thomas).

This clan traces its ancestry to Tómaidh Mór (big Tommy), bastard son of Angus, sixth chief of Clan MacKintosh, who in the mid-fourteenth century migrated from Inverness-shire to Glen Shee in Perthshire (the name appears as MacThomas, MacComish, McCombie, or MacComie). The chiefship passed in 1600 to John MacComie of Finegand. During the religious wars he supported the Stuarts against the Covenanters, but during the Commonwealth switched sides and suffered at the Restoration. The family lost their estates in 1676 and moved to Angus and Fife, anglicizing their surname as Thom, Thomas, or Thomson.

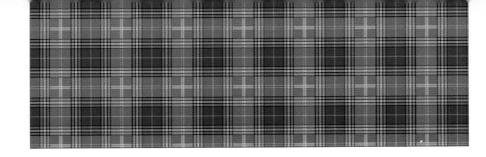

MACWHIRTER

Gaelic: *Mac Chruiter* (Son of the harper)

This surname derives from a trade—harpers were indispensable retainers and no chiefly household would have been complete without the resident harpist. This role was passed from father to son and in view of the hereditary nature of the appointment, it invariably entailed a grant of land. The harpers in royal households, of course, were at the top of the tree, and it is from the royal harpers who acquired the estate of Dalelachane in the mid-fourteenth century that the Clan MacWhirter is descended. Variants of the name include MacGruder and MacGrowther as well as the common anglicized form, Harper. Famous bearers of these names include Alexander McWhorter (1734–1807), a founder of Princeton College; the artist John MacWhirter; the brothers Ross and Norris McWhirter, who created the *Guinness Book of World Records*; and James Harper (1795–1869), founder of the publishing house.

MACWILLIAM

Gaelic: *Mac Uilleim* (Son of William)

William as a forename was unknown in Scotland before the late eleventh century, but in 1094 Duncan, son of Malcolm III by his first wife, Ingibiorg, returned to Scotland from exile in England (where he had been held hostage by the Conqueror since 1072). He briefly ousted his uncle, Donald Bane, before he met his death at Mondynes the same year, leaving an illegitimate son, William, the progenitor of the clan. The principal line came to a sticky end in 1215 when the baby heiress of the MacWilliam chief was battered to death against the market cross in Forfar. As this surname later became a common patronymic, it, and its anglicized version Williamson, is widespread, although MacWilliam families were offshoots of the MacLeods and the Robertsons in the sixteenth and seventeenth centuries, and were later regarded as septs of the MacFarlanes, Gunns, or MacPhersons.

MAITLAND

Badge: A lion sejant holding a sword, with
the Latin motto *Consilio et animis* (By
counsel and reasoning)

This powerful Lowland family originated in
Normandy and came to Scotland a couple of
generations after the Conquest, via estates in
Northumberland. The earliest reference to this
family in Scotland occurs in a document witnessed
by Thomas de Maltalent in 1227. Sir Richard de
Mauteland acquired the Berwickshire estate of
Thirlestane later in the same century and around
1345 his descendant added Lethington in East
Lothian. Several generations held high office,
notably William (c. 1528–73), who was principal
secretary to Mary, Queen of Scots; his brother
John (1545–95), the chancellor who was raised to
the peerage; and his grandson John (1616–82),
who became Duke of Lauderdale in 1672.

MALCOLM

Badge: A silver tower, with the Latin motto
In ardua petit (He aims at difficult things)
Gaelic: *Mac Mhaol Chaluim*

The name means "son of the devotee of St.
Columba" and shows the close connections with
the MacCallums, but the name Malcolm was
adopted in 1779 when Dugald MacCallum
succeeded to the estate of Poltalloch, and John
Malcolm of Poltalloch was named Lord Malcolm in
1896. A branch of the Malcolms has been
domiciled in Stirlingshire since the fourteenth
century.

MAR

Badge: Ten feathers on a cap, with the
    phonetic French motto *Pans plus*
    (Think more)
Gaelic: *Màr*

This clan derives its name from the lands of Mar, one of the seven ancient divisions of Scotland ruled by mormaers (governors) who later became Earls of Mar. Rothri, the first earl, was named in a charter of Scone Abbey in 1114, while John, the twenty-third earl, was named Duke of Mar by the Old Pretender (James VIII), though his estates and titles were forfeited for his part in the first Jacobite Rebellion in 1715. The earldom was eventually restored to John, the twenty-fourth earl, in 1824. The present holder of the title is Countess of Mar in her own right. A separate earldom, of Mar and Kellie, is held by the Erskine family and dates from 1565. Variant spellings are Marr and Mair.

MATHESON

Badge: A forearm wielding a sword, with the
    Latin motto *Fac et spera* (Do and hope)
Gaelic: *MacMhathain*

Known as the Clan of the Bear, this ancient Celtic family held lands in Wester Ross and Sutherland. The story goes that they aided Kenneth MacAlpin in gaining the Pictish throne in 843. In more recent times the two main branches were the Mathesons of Lochalsh and Shiness, from whom Sir Alexander and Sir James are descendents, respectively, both baronets who made vast fortunes in India and spent their money on estates in Ross-shire and Lewis. The latter, Sir James, was cofounder of Jardine Matheson of Hong Kong, now recognized as a global conglomerate.

MAXWELL

Badge: A stag in front of a holly bush, with
the Latin motto *Reviresco* (I grow strong
again)

The name of this powerful Border family is derived
from Maccus Well on the River Tweed near Kelso,
named after a Saxon nobleman with estates in the
eastern Borders. The family itself is of Norman
origin and settled in Scotland in the twelfth century.
By 1241 Sir John Maxwell was Chamberlain of
Scotland, followed by his brother Aymer, whose
sons Herbert and John were the progenitors of the
many branches of the family widespread
throughout the Borders, from Galloway to
Roxburghshire. Herbert Maxwell was raised to the
peerage in 1445 and from him sprang Lord Herries,
the earldom of Nithsdale, and the baronetcies of
Cardoness, Monreith, Springkell, and Pollok, as
well as numerous lairdships in Dumfries and
Galloway. Most famous of the name are the
physicist James Clerk Maxwell (1831–79) and
Stirling Maxwell, chief British prosecutor at the
Nuremberg Trials. On the other hand, the most
notorious, the publisher Robert Maxwell (1923–91),
was born Ludvik Hoch and only assumed the name
on settling in Britain.

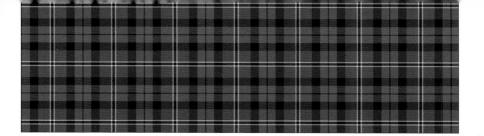

MELVILLE

Badge: A lion's head, with the Latin motto
Denique coelum (The sky, at last)

Guillaume de Malleville accompanied William the Conqueror in 1066 and his descendants migrated to Scotland early in the twelfth century, Galfridus de Malvell becoming Sheriff of Edinburgh in 1162. Never far from the seat of power, the Melvilles rose to prominence in the sixteenth century and held high offices of state under James V and Mary, Queen of Scots. Sir Robert Melville was raised to the peerage in 1616. George, fourth Lord Melville (1636–1707), was implicated in the Monmouth Rebellion of 1685 and fled to the European continent. He returned with William of Orange (1689), became president of the Privy Council, and received an earldom. His son David also inherited the title Earl of Leven through his mother. The most famous holders of the name were the religious reformer Andrew Melville (1545–1622) and the novelist Herman Melville (1819–91).

MENZIES

Badge: A full-face savage head, with the
    motto "Will God I shall"
Gaelic: *Meinnearach*

The progenitor of this clan was a Norman
mercenary named de Meyners, whose descendant,
Robert, became Lord High Chamberlain in 1249
and held lands in Perthshire. The letter "z" is actually
the medieval letter yogh, pronounced like a "y" or
"g," so the correct pronunciation of this name
should be "Mingies." Menzies of Culdares
introduced the larch and the monkey puzzle tree to
Scotland in the 1730s. The most famous clansman
with this name was Sir Robert Menzies, Prime
Minister of Australia.

MERRILEES

Sir Walter Scott's romance *Guy Mannering*, in
which the young hero Harry Bertram is kidnapped
and robbed of his inheritance by a rascally lawyer,
captured the imagination of readers everywhere in
the years following its publication in 1815. The
central character in the novel was a very
resourceful gypsy named Meg Merrilees, who
identifies the young man and helps him recover his
estates. She became a rather unlikely heroine in
the mold of Flora MacDonald, and this inspired a
weaver to produce this tartan, named in her honor.
Scott's novels went out of fashion and few people
now remember Meg Merrilees, whose tartan was
later appropriated by people of this surname. The
main action of the novel takes place in
Dumfriesshire, still the home of people named
Merrilees or Mirrlees. Most famous of this name is
James Mirrlees, winner of the Nobel Prize for
Economics in 1996.

MIDDLETON

Badge: A wild man holding an uprooted
   tree, with the Latin motto *Fortis in arduis*
   (Strong in adversity)

The name derives from the estate of Middleton, near Laurencekirk in Kincardineshire, which was granted to Malcolm by King Duncan II in 1094. In 1238, Humphrey de Middleton witnessed a charter of Arbroath Abbey while his namesake signed the Ragman Rolls in 1296. John Middleton of Caldhame (1608–74) rose to prominence in the ranks of the Covenanters, but later changed sides and fought for Charles II at Worcester (1651). At the Restoration he was named Earl of Middleton and was later governor of Tangier. The earldom was forfeited when the second earl supported the Jacobite cause. Two of his sons later became successive principals of King's College, Aberdeen. Famous persons of this surname include the Jacobean playwright Thomas Middleton (1570–1627), the actress Noelle Middleton, and the writer John Middleton Murry (1889–1957).

MOFFAT

Badge: A winged spur, with the Latin
   motto *Nunquam non paratus* (Never
   unprepared)

This name derives from the Dumfriesshire town, nestling amid the mountains near the source of the Annan and the Tweed and long famous for its chalybeate springs, which made it a popular spa in the eighteenth and nineteenth centuries. It has a long history as a center of the wool industry and became a royal burgh in 1648. A tartan with a red ground may have been created as a civic tartan, but a tartan specific to the clan was designed as recently as 1983 to celebrate the revival of the chiefship after a gap of 420 years. Nicholas de Mufet was Archdeacon of Teviotdale in 1245, while Robert de Moffat was Church Treasurer of Glasgow in 1436. The ecclesiastical connection continued in the nineteenth century with Robart Moffat (1795–1883), the African missionary and father-in-law of David Livingstone, and James Moffatt (1870–1944), the theologian who translated the Bible into modern English.

MONCREIFFE

Badge: A demi-lion issuing from a coronet, with the French motto *Sur esperance* (Upon hope)

Gaelic: *Monadh craoibhe* (Hill of the sacred bough)

The name of this clan derives from a barony near Perth, whose hill was an important site for the pagan Picts associated with Druidism (the worship of oak trees). The clan claims descent from the priestly rulers of Pictland—both Duncan I (1034–40) and Niall of the Nine Hostages are among their ancestors. However, the earliest actual record of the name is the charter of 1248 from Alexander II to Sir Matthew de Muncrephe. The three principal branches of the clan descend from the eighth laird in the fifteenth century: the Moncreiffes of Moncreiffe, Tulliebole, and Bandirran. Sir David Moncreiffe, the twenty-third laird, perished in the fire that destroyed the family seat in 1957. His nephew and successor was Sir Iain Moncreiffe, the noted historian, genealogist, and expert on Scottish heraldry.

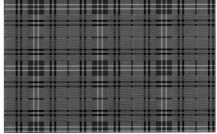

MONTGOMERY

Badge: A female figure holding a savage's
    head and an anchor, with the French
    motto *Gardez bien* (Look well)
Gaelic: *MacGumerait*

Originally a Norman family from the Falaise district,
the Montgomerys descend from Roger de
Montgomery, regent of Normandy, who came with
the Conqueror and was named an earl. His
grandson, Robert, came to Scotland with Walter
the Steward and received the lands of Eaglesham
from David I. A peerage in the fifteenth century
became the earldom of Eglinton in 1507, and the
family possessed considerable estates in Ayrshire
and Renfrewshire. Famous clansmen with this
name are Richard Montgomery, a general in the
American War for Independence, and Field Marshal
Viscount Montgomery of Alamein.

MORRISON

Badge: A coiled serpent, with the Latin
    motto *Praetia prudentia praestat* (In price,
    prudence predominates)
Gaelic: *MacGhille Mhoire*

Despite the Gaelic name, rendered variously as
"son of Maurice" or "son of the servant of the Virgin
Mary," this clan is descended from Vikings
shipwrecked on the shores of Lewis. The
Morrisons of Habost were hereditary breves
(lawyers) as late as the seventeenth century when
they turned to the church. Although Morrisons are
still plentiful in Lewis, branches of the clan settled
in Harris, Uist, Skye, and Sutherland, but the
Morrisons of Dunbartonshire, Perthshire, and
Stirling are believed to have been a separate family.
The most famous members of the clan are Marion
Morrison (1907–79, aka John Wayne), and the
musician Jim Morrison (1943–71) of The Doors.

MOWAT

This surname derives from the French *mont hault* or *haut* (high mount), Latinized in early charters as *de monte alto*. It first appears in Scotland in the reign of David I (1124–53) with the arrival of Robert Montealto, a Norman knight who had previously been granted lands in Wales. Robert de Muheut is named in a charter of about 1210 while William de Montealto took part in the survey of Arbroath Abbey in 1219 and Michael de Montealto was Sheriff of Inverness in 1234. Later the family obtained estates in Angus and Ayrshire, where the surname is still common. Variants of the surname include Mouat, Mowatt, and Mott. Most famous of the clan was Axel Mowat (1593–1661), Admiral of Norway, and Sir Oliver Mowat (1820–1903), Canadian statesman.

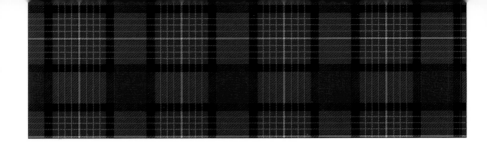

MUIR

Badge: A Moor's head, with the Latin motto *Durum patientia frango* (By patience I break that which is hard)

Gaelic: *Moire* (The Virgin Mary) or *Mór* (Big)

Despite the Gaelic derivations and the red herring of the Moor's head, this surname probably derives from people who lived on or near moorland. The earliest recorded ancestor was Gilchrist Mure, who won his spurs at Largs in 1263. His son Archibald was killed in the massacre of Berwick in 1290. Thomas de la More was named as the executor of Devorgilla Balliol, mother of King John, in 1291, but the family's royal connections really took off in 1346 when the future Robert II married Elizabeth, daughter of Sir Adam Mure of Rowallan, the mother of Robert III and ancestress of the Stewart dynasty. The male line of the Muirs of Rowallan died out in 1700, but cadet branches included the Muirs of Cassencarie and Deanston. Variants include Mure and Moir, regarded as septs of the Gordons. Famous persons include the poet Edwin Muir (1887–1959), the fashion designer Jean Muir (1933–95), and the pioneer conservationist John Muir (1838–1914).

MUNRO

Badge: A spread eagle, with the motto
  "Dread God"
Gaelic: *Mac an Rothaich*

The founder of this clan is said to have come from Roe in County Derry, but the earliest Munro on record is Hugh of Foulis, who died in 1126. Robert Foulis supported Bruce at Bannockburn, and thereafter the clan was closely associated with the crown. In the seventeenth century the clan featured prominently in European wars, providing three generals and thirteen colonels for the armies of Gustavus Adolphus, as well as numerous officers of lesser rank. Famous clansmen include Sir Thomas Munro, a noted Indian administrator, and James Monroe, fifth president of the United States. Also, a "munro" is a Scottish peak over 3,000 ft., from Sir Hugh Munro, who classified them in 1891.

MURRAY

Badge: A demi-savage holding a dagger,
  with the motto "Furth fortune and fill the
  fetters"
Gaelic: *MacMhuirich*

This powerful clan had its origins in the Celtic tribes of Moray but later acquired lands all over Scotland. Sir Andrew Moray was Wallace's chief lieutenant in the Battle of Stirling Bridge. Sir John of Tullibardine was named Lord Murray (1604) and Earl of Tullibardine (1606). His grandson claimed the earldom of Atholl (1629), and later raised to a dukedom. Marriage with an heiress of the Stanley Earls of Derby brought the Isle of Man. John, the third duke, sold his title of Lord of Man to the crown in 1765. Other branches of the clan included the Earls of Dunmore and Mansfield.

MURRAY OF ATHOLL

Gaelic: *Mac Mhuirich*

The marriage of William Murray, second Earl of Tullibardine, to Dorothea Stewart, heiress of Atholl, in 1629 brought the premier branch of the clan to national prominence. The title was raised to a marquessate in 1676 and finally a dukedom in 1703. Blair Castle, the family seat, is one of the largest and most sumptuous mansions In Scotland, parts of it dating from 1269. This strategic stronghold was occupied by Montrose in 1644, Claverhouse in 1689, and the Duke of Cumberland in 1746 when it was badly damaged, ironically as a result of the artillery of Lord George Murray, commander of the Jacobite forces, who laid siege to his family home. James, the second duke, minted his own coins as Lord of Man (1758), and to this day the Duke of Atholl is the only peer of the realm allowed to have his own private army, the Atholl Highlanders.

MURRAY OF TULLIBARDINE

Gaelic: *Mac Mhuirich*

This branch of the clan is descended from William de Moravia, a grandson of Freskin the Pict, who was appointed mormaor (governor) of Moray by David I early in the twelfth century. One of William's sons married the heiress of Tullibardine, a district in Perthshire six miles south of Crieff. It possesses the finest collegiate church in Scotland, built in 1445 by Sir David Murray. Sir John Murray, twelfth of Tullibardine, was made an earl by James VI in 1606.

His grandson married the heiress of the Stewart Earls of Atholl and his descendants became Marquesses and, later, Dukes of Atholl; the courtesy title Marquess of Tullibardine is used by the duke's eldest son to this day. From the Tullibardine line came William Murray (1600–51), named Earl of Dysart (1643); Lord Charles Murray (1661–1710), later first Earl of Dunmore; and William Murray, Lord Chief Justice and first Earl of Mansfield (1776).

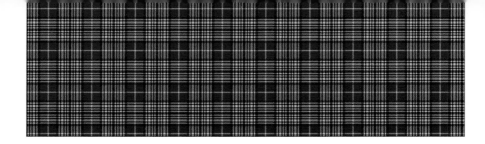

NAPIER

Badge: A right hand grasping an eagle's leg, with the Latin motto *Vincit veritas* (Truth prevails)

The name, which has no Gaelic equivalent, derives from an ancestor who was in charge of the royal linen. John de Napier held lands in Dunbartonshire by the late thirteenth century and his descendants were prominent in the royal service, notably Sir Alexander of Merchiston, who was Comptroller to James II, Lord Provost of Edinburgh, Vice-Admiral of Scotland, and ambassador to England at various times. Famous clansmen include John of Merchiston, inventor of logarithms, and General Lord Napier of Magdala.

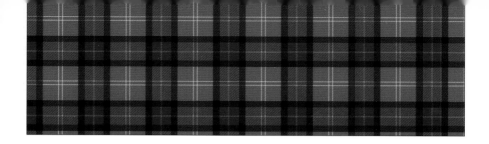

NESBITT

Badge: A black boar, with the motto "I byde it"

This Border family derives its name from the barony of Nesbit in Berwickshire, although it may also come from the village of Nisbet four miles north of Jedburgh, in Roxburghshire. The surname is variously spelled Nesbit, Nesbitt, Nisbet, or Nisbett. The earliest mention of the name occurs in a charter of Coldingham priory around 1160, witnessed by William de Nesbite. Adam Nisbet of Nisbet was granted the estate of Knocklies by Robert the Bruce. Philip Nisbet fought for the Covenanters in the wars of the seventeenth century, whereas John Nisbet of Dirleton (1609–87) was the Lord Advocate who led the persecution of the Covenanters in the reign of Charles II, who raised him to the peerage as Lord Dirleton. Most famous of the clan is children's novelist Edith Nesbit, who wrote *The Railway Children* and the fantasy *The Phoenix and the Carpet.*

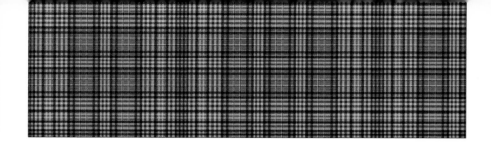

OGILVIE

Badge: A woman holding a portcullis, with the French motto *Á fin* (To the end)

Gaelic: *MacGhille Bhuidhe*

Gilbert, second son of Gilchrist, Earl of Angus, received the barony of Ogilvie from William the Lyon in 1163. His descendants became hereditary sheriffs of Angus and built the tower of Airlie. From a cadet of this family originated the Earls of Findlater and Seafield and Lords of Banff. Sir James Ogilvie of Airlie was named Lord Airlie in 1491 and this was advanced to an earldom in 1639 but attainted in 1746 and not restored until 1826. Sir Angus Ogilvy, younger son of the ninth earl, married Her Royal Highness Princess Alexandra of Kent in 1963.

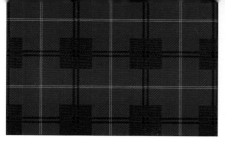

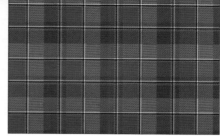

OLIPHANT

Badge: A gold crescent, with the motto
"What was may be"

The name is derived from the elephant, symbolic of immense strength, and is derived from the Norman David de Olifard, who came to Scotland in the retinue of David I in 1141. Sir Lawrence Oliphant was raised to the peerage in 1458. Later Oliphants of Gask were staunch supporters of the Jacobite cause. Carolina Oliphant (1766–1844), named after Prince Charles, is best remembered under her married name as Lady Nairne, the Scottish songwriter. This clan shares its tartan with the Melvilles, descended from another Norman in the entourage of David I who took his name from the manor of Mala Ville.

OLYMPIC

From 776 B.C. until the fourth century A.D., athletes from all over the Greek world came together every four years at Olympia to test their strength and skills. During the Olympic Games, all wars were suspended. It was the Olympic ideal of uniting mankind through sport that inspired Baron Pierre de Coubertin to revive the Games. The first such event of modern times was staged at Athens in 1896. The fifth Olympiad was held at White City, London, in 1912, and the Games returned to England in 1948. Although Scotland has never hosted the Olympic Games, it has produced a number of gold medalists, most notably the runner Eric Liddell (1902–45), whose story was the basis for the film *Chariots of Fire*. The Olympic tartan, embodying the colors of the Olympic rings, was devised in 1984. In the original version the rings themselves were included on the red ground, but were later omitted.

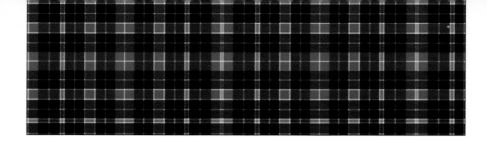

ORDER OF THE HOLY SEPULCHRE OF JERUSALEM

Godfrey of Bouillon (c. 1061–1100), Duke of Lower Lorraine, was the leader of the First Crusade. After the capture of Jerusalem from the Saracens in 1099, he was proclaimed king but refused the crown, accepting only the title of Defender of the Holy Sepulchre. Although he died soon afterward, his example of chivalry inspired the creation of the order of monastic knights, which, like the Hospitallers and the Templars, gave spiritual and physical support to pilgrims in the Holy Land. In its modern guise, the Order is primarily a charity engaged in humanitarian projects. The tartan, approved by the Lieutenant of the Order in Scotland, was designed in 1990 by Ronald Kinsey, who based it on Wilson's Priests or Clergy sett, although the colors symbolize Jerusalem (yellow and white), the Crusaders (red and white), and the Canons Regular at the Holy Sepulchre (black).

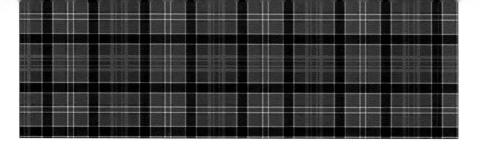

PAISLEY

Badge: A mitered abbot flanked by
cinquefoils, with the motto "Lord, let Paisley
flourish by the preaching of Thy word"

Gaelic: *Paislig*

This is a district tartan, created only recently, in 1952, when Allan C. Drennan, assistant manager of a department store in the town, won a design competition at the Royal Highland Show in Kelso. Its colors are derived from those of the civic arms. The town developed around the Abbey founded in 1163 by Walter Fitz Alan, progenitor of the Royal Stewarts (through his descendant Walter the Steward, who married Marjorie Bruce, daughter of King Robert I). The town profited from the Industrial Revolution and became a leading textile center, particularly noted for its shawls, whose distinctive patterns were derived from silks sent home by Scots in the service of the East India Company. The tartan has also become popular with persons of the surname, many of whom migrated to Ulster in the seventeenth and eighteenth centuries and include Dr. Ian Paisley, the militant Protestant clergyman and political leader.

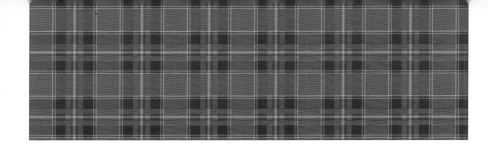

PERTHSHIRE

Badge: A Highlander armed with claymore and targe, with the Latin motto *Pro lege et libertate* (For law and liberty)

Gaelic: *Peart*

Scholars are divided regarding the derivation of this name, some arguing that it is Welsh (or Brythonic), meaning "bush" or "copse," while others consider it to be a corruption of Abertay, through Bertha to Perth. Perthshire lies at the very heart of Scotland, hence the expression *"fo Hiort gu Peart"* ("from St. Kilda to Perth," the Gaelic equivalent of the English phrase "from Land's End to John O'Groats," meaning from one end of the country to the other). The city straddles the River Tay, Scotland's longest river, which traverses the county from its source in Loch Tay to its estuary. Known as the Fair City, Perth and its surrounding district were at the very heart of Pictland; the Kings of Scots were traditionally crowned at nearby Scone, while Dunkeld in the same county was one of the spiritual capitals of Scotland. The district tartan, derived from that of the Drummonds, was first recorded by Wilson's of Bannockburn in 1831 when it was described as Perthshire Rock and Wheel (a type of soft tartan). Two variants were subsequently designed in the 1990s.

PRIDE OF SCOTLAND

This is one of the latest universal or all-purpose trade tartans, designed by D. C. Dalgleish for McCall's of Aberdeen and intended mainly for the kilt-hire business as the fashion for tartan at weddings and other functions escalates. The colors of this sett were apparently inspired by the film *Braveheart*, Mel Gibson's highly fictionalized account of the life and death of the patriot William Wallace, although it should be noted that there are three universal tartans of that name as well.

PRINCE OF WALES

Lochcarron of Galashiels created this trade tartan in 1998; although named in honor of Prince Charles, Duke of Rothesay, it can be worn by anyone, on the same analogy as the Royal Stewart tartan. The red, green, and white colors are derived from the distinctive Welsh flag, which was only officially adopted by the Principality in 1911 at the time of the Investiture of Prince David, eldest son of King George V and the future Edward VIII, the first Prince of Wales to be installed in more than a century. The title of Prince of Wales, borne by the eldest son of the monarch, was created at the end of the thirteenth century by King Edward I, who, before he became the Hammer of the Scots, had already beaten the Welsh into subjugation. Ironically, it was Welsh archers that saved the day for the English at the Battle of Falkirk in 1298.

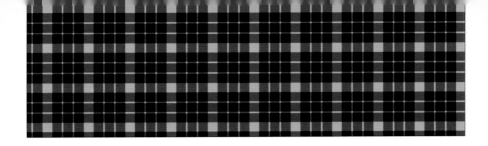

RAEBURN

Badge: A stag's head, with the Latin motto
   Tutis fortis (Safe if strong)

This surname has been traced back to the Rye or Rae Burn in the Ayrshire parish of Dunlop, and is first recorded in a document of 1331 witnessed by William of Raeburn. By the fifteenth century it was a relatively common surname, with various spellings, including Ryburn, Reburne, and Raburn, in the Glasgow area. The most famous person of this name was Sir Henry Raeburn (1756–1823). Born near Edinburgh, he worked as a portrait miniaturist in watercolors but later graduated to full-scale oil paintings. After studying in Rome, he returned to Edinburgh, where he was one of the most fashionable portraitists of his day and was knighted in 1822 during the state visit of King George IV to Edinburgh. What Sir Walter Scott did in words, Raeburn did in oils to popularize the wearing of tartan among the upper classes, and the setts depicted so accurately in many of his paintings have proved an invaluable historical record to the early years of the modern resurgence of tartan.

RAMSAY

RANGERS F.C.

Badge: A unicorn's head, with the Latin motto *Ora et labora* (Pray and work)

Norman Simon de Ramsay was granted estates in Lothian by David I and founded the family of Dalhousie. Raised to the peerage in 1618, the Dalhousies advanced to an earldom in 1633. Successive generations had illustrious military careers. James, the tenth earl, was named Marquess of Dalhousie in 1849 and served as Governor General of India and Canada. He died in 1860 without issue and his titles passed to his cousin, the second Lord Panmure. Famous clansmen include the poet Allan Ramsay and Sir William Ramsay, awarded the Nobel Prize in chemistry in 1904.

Rangers is one of the oldest soccer clubs in Scotland; its rival in the "Old Firm" being Celtic. Although some form of soccer was being played in Scotland since the Middle Ages, it was not until the 1870s that Scotland adopted the rules laid down by the newly formed Football Association (hence "soccer"). Rangers was founded in 1873 by a group of amateur oarsmen at Gareloch on the Firth of Clyde. While Celtic is predominantly Catholic, Rangers was an exclusively Protestant club, its staunch adherence to the Crown reflected in its royal blue shirts with white and red trim, which are reflected in the club tartan. This was the first of a series of soccer club tartans developed by the Glasgow firm of John MacGregor, and it was formally launched by Ally McCoist in September 1989. Tartan Sportswear, the company set up to develop sporting tartans, was succeeded by Geoffrey (Tailor) Highland Crafts in 1994.

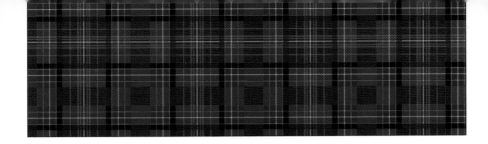

RANKIN

Badge: A cubit arm brandishing a battle-ax

This surname is believed to have arisen from the diminutive form of Randy (short for Randoph or Bertrand) and is known also as a forename from the fifteenth century onward. Peter Rankyne of the Scheild was witness to a document at Kilmarnock in 1504 and other persons of the same or similar names have been recorded in Ayrshire charters and writs from the middle of the fifteenth century. The hamlet of Rankinston, near Ayr, derives its name from this family. There was also, at one time, a Castle Rankine, which has long since vanished, although it lent its name to a prisoner of war camp in the 1940s. Famous persons of this name include the Australian stateswoman Dame Annabella Rankin (1908–86), the American feminist and pacificist Jeanneatte Rankin (1880–1973), the novelist Ian Rankin, and the pioneer of thermodynamics, Sir William Rankine (1820–75).

RATTRAY

Badge: A radiant heart surmounting a five-pointed star rising out of a coronet, with the Latin motto *Super sidera votum* (A desire beyond the stars)

Pictish: *Rath-tref* (Fortified dwelling)

This is one of the few place-names in Scotland (other than those with the prefix Pit or Pen) that have definitely been derived from the aboriginal Celtic language that disappeared with the coming of the Scots in the late sixth century. It gave the name to a small barony in Perthshire, whose landholders were well-documented from the early thirteenth century under various names such as Rethereth and Retref. John Rattray, the eleventh laird, was knighted by James IV in 1488 but perished at Flodden in 1513. His younger son Patrick was persecuted and eventually murdered by John Stewart, second Earl of Atholl and his niece Grizel forced to marry the third earl. The family was restored to its estates in 1648, Patrick, the eighteenth laird, being granted the barony of Craighall-Rattray. Later generations served in India, where Rattray's Light Horse was a cavalry regiment.

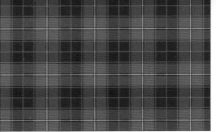

RENNIE

This name, sometimes spelled Rainy, Renny, or Rainey, arose from a diminutive form of the forenames Reynold or Reginald, which seem to have been particularly popular in the Craig district of Angus, although landholders of these surnames have also been recorded as far afield as Fife and Aberdeenshire from 1362 onward. In fact, the former royal burgh of Kilrenny, in Fife, points to the existence of some Celtic saint of this name. Famous persons of this name include the actor Michael Rennie and the architect and civil engineer John Rennie (1761–1821), who built many of the great bridges of Britain in the early nineteenth century, notably London Bridge (now at Lake Havasu, Arizona). It was also the middle name of the celebrated architect and interior designer, Charles Rennie Mackintosh (1868–1933), his mother's maiden name.

ROBERTSON

Badge: A hand holding an imperial crown, with the Latin motto *Virtutis gloria merces* (Glory is the reward of valor)
Gaelic: *MacDhonnachaidh*

The Clan Donnachaidh claims descent from the Celtic Earls of Atholl and derives its name from Donnachadh Reamhar (Stout Duncan), who led the clan to victory at Bannockburn, though the name Robertson comes from his descendant Robert Riach (grizzled), who apprehended the assassins of James I and was rewarded with the barony of Struan in 1451. The clan was an ardent supporter of the Stewarts throughout the civil wars and Jacobite uprisings. Sir William Robertson enlisted as a private soldier and rose to the rank of field marshal in World War I.

ROBERTSON OF KINDEACE

The Scottish Tartans Society lists no fewer than a dozen tartans for Clan Robertson, although it comments that one is a "phantom" (by Dalgleish) and another is "wildly wrong," illustrating the problems of distinguishing the authentic from the modern or the frankly spurious. The majority of tartans have a red ground and belong in the group of Robertson of Struan, the senior line, but a distinctive tartan, familiarly known as "Hunting Robertson," has a predominantly green and blue ground. It is of immense antiquity and was worn by the Robertsons of Kindeace, the northerly branch of the clan, whose lands were at Kindeace, near Tain in Easter Ross. It was first recorded in the Cockburn Collection (1810–15), which is now preserved in the Mitchell Library in Glasgow.

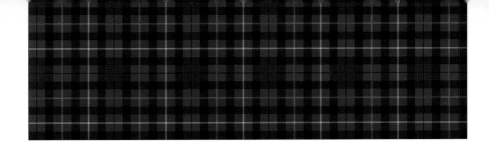

ROLLO

Badge: A stag's head, with the French motto
La fortune passé partout (Fortune makes
way through everything)

This small clan derives its name from Hrolf Ganger (Rollo the Walker), a Viking chief who was such a giant of a man that he could not find a horse strong enough to bear him and therefore had to "gang" on foot. In the early tenth century he led a number of audacious raids on western Europe and even sailed up the Seine to besiege Paris. In 911, Charles III of France bought him off with the Duchy of Normandy. His direct descendant was Duke William, who conquered England in 1066. One of his kinsmen and closest supporters was Erik Rollo, whose grandson moved to Scotland in 1124 and is recorded in documents of 1141 as Rollo or Rollok. John Rollo, secretary to the Earl of Strathearn, received the estate of Duncrub, Perthshire, in 1380. Sir Andrew Rollo of Duncrub became the first Lord Rollo in 1651 for services in the civil war.

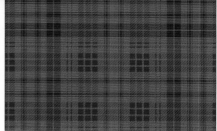

ROSE

Badge: A harp, with the motto "Constant and true"

Gaelic: *Rois*

This clan of Norman origins takes its name from the flower and was settled in Strathnairn by the late twelfth century. Hugh Rose married the heiress of Kilravock, which has been the clan seat ever since. Invariably supporting whichever government was in power, the Roses avoided the fate of so many others in the eighteenth century. The most famous clansman was Sir Hugh Rose, a veteran of many Indian campaigns, who rose to become a field marshal and was named Baron Strathnairn in 1866. J. A. Rose, a high official in the French Revolution, organized an escape route for émigrés and was the original Scarlet Pimpernel.

ROSS

Badge: A right hand holding a laurel crown, with the Latin motto *Spem successus alit* (Success feeds hope)

Gaelic: *Ros*

Recent thinking suggests that this clan, like Clan Rose, had a common Norman ancestry, although traditionally it is regarded as being one of the oldest Celtic families, taking its name from the ancient province of Ross. The progenitor of the clan is regarded as Fearchar Mac-an-t-sagairt (son of the priest), Laird of Applecross, who was named Earl of Ross in 1234. William, the third earl, led the clan at Bannockburn. The clan is also known as Clan Andrias, from MacGhille Aindreas, a chief predating the earldom, which passed to the Lords of the Isles in 1424. The chiefship then passed to Hugh Ross (or Rariches), whose family acquired Balnagowan.

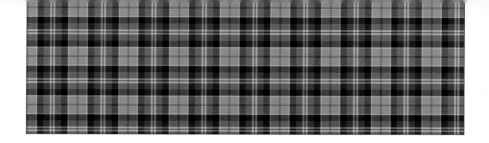

ROTHESAY

Badge: A lymphad (galley), triple-towered
   castle, crescent, and tenny star on one
   side and a fess chequy on the other,
   without a motto

Gaelic: *Rothasaidh*

The largest town on the island of Bute and former capital of the county of that name (including Arran and Cumbrae), Rothesay is one of the most popular holiday resorts in the Firth of Clyde. It was raised to the status of a royal burgh in 1401 by Robert III, who conferred the title of Duke of Rothesay on his eldest son. Since that time it has been the premier Scottish title of the heir to the throne and, as such, is enjoyed by the Prince of Wales to this day. He is often referred to in Scotland by this title and two of the seven Rothesay tartans are reserved for his exclusive use. Rothesay Castle, dating from 1098, was the chief Norse stronghold in the Firth until the defeat of Haakon V at Largs in 1263. Of the four district tartans, a predominantly red one derived from the Royal Stewart sett was habitually worn by the future Edward VII as a boy and appears to predate the Duke of Rothesay tartans of the present day. The most common of the district tartans has a predominantly gray and brown pattern.

ROY, ROB

This is one of the oldest tartans, a specimen of the sett having been collected as long ago as 1815–16 by the Highland Society of London. From this it appears that it was designed for the baronet, Sir John MacGregor Murray of MacGregor. It takes its name from the celebrated Highland plunderer, much romanticized by Sir Walter Scott's novel of 1817 and a popular figure in Scottish mythology ever since. There was, of course, a real Rob Roy (Red Robert) MacGregor, born in the Buchanan district of Stirlingshire in 1671. A law-abiding grazier, he was cheated by the first Duke of Montrose in 1712 and turned to cattle-rustling under the protection of Montrose's arch enemy, the Duke of Argyll. Distrusted by both sides during the Jacobite Rebellion of 1715, he was eventually captured in 1722, sentenced to exile in Barbados, but freed from a London prison before the order was carried out, allegedly on the intervention of his feisty wife, Helen. He returned to Scotland in 1727 and died there in 1734. A Rob Roy hunting tartan also exists, originally known as Robin Hood.

ROYAL AND ANCIENT

The Fife town of St. Andrews boasts four full-length golf courses. Of these, the New Course, the Eden, and the Jubilee are mere youngsters compared to the Old Course, on which golf has been played since the fifteenth century, although the Royal and Ancient Golf Club, the oldest and most prestigious in the world, was not formally established until 1754. Its splendid buildings were erected exactly a century later, but as the club approaches its 250th anniversary, it was in need of extensive refurbishment. By the 1990s, the notion of a tartan as a fund-raising device was well established and thus this tartan was created in 1993 by Kinloch Anderson of Leith. Its predominant green and blue shades reflect its royal status as well as the vivid color of the course itself.

ROYAL STEWART

Badge: A seated lion holding a sword and
   scepter, with the motto "In defens"
Gaelic: *Stiubhard*

The royal clan is descended from Walter fitz Alan, appointed hereditary Steward by David I, with extensive lands in Renfrewshire. Walter, sixth Steward, married Marjorie Bruce, daughter of Robert I, and founded the dynasty, which continues to this day. From the first three sons of Walter's uncle, Sir John Stewart of Bonkill, came the great earldoms of Angus, Lennox, and Galloway. The Stewarts also hold, or held, the dukedoms of Rothesay (now held by Prince Charles), Albany, and Lennox, the marquessate of Bute, and the earldoms of Atholl, Buchan, Carrick, Menteith, and Strathearn, as well as numerous lesser titles. Forty-eight tartans pertaining to this clan are recorded by the Scottish Tartans Society (*see* Stewart).

RUSSELL

Badge: A hand holding a sword centered
under a balance, with the Latin motto
Virtus sine macula (Virtue without stain)

Various French towns, such as Roussel and Rosel, have been suggested as the origins of this clan, whose progenitor "came with the Conqueror," although it is probable that many bearers of the modern surname were descended from an ancestor who acquired a nickname alluding to his red hair or ruddy complexion. This explains the very widespread appearance of the surname in Scottish records from the middle of the twelfth century onward. The Russells of Aberdeenshire, however, trace their descent from an Anglo-Norman knight who fought on the English side at Halidon Hill (1333) before moving north. The Russells are regarded as a sept of the Cummings. The surname is also very common in England and borne by many prominent families from the time of John Russell, first Earl of Bedford (1486–1555). The tartan shown here is the same as Galbraith and Hunter. It was first known as Galbraith in the collection of the Highland Society of London, but William Wilson and Sons of Bannockburn recorded the pattern as Russell in their pattern book of 1847, although it was named Hunter in an earlier book of 1819.

RUTHVEN

Badge: A ram's head with the Scots motto
   Deid schaw (Deeds show)

Gaelic: *Roth-bheinn* (Wheel hill)

This place-name occurs in several parts of Scotland, notably in Aberdeenshire, Inverness-shire, and Perthshire, although the family of this name derives from the barony of Ruthven in Tayside, where the progenitor of the clan, a Viking marauder named Sweyn Thorsson, settled in the eleventh century. His grandson, Sir Walter Ruthven, is recorded around 1235, while the lands in Perthshire were granted to his descendant in 1298. Sir William was raised to the peerage in 1487 and it was his grandson Patrick (1520–66) who rose from his deathbed to strike the first blow in the murder of David Riccio, Queen Mary's favorite. William, fourth Lord Ruthven and first Earl of Gowrie, was Mary's jailer at Lochleven, but was involved in the kidnapping of James VI (the Ruthven Raid, 1582). John, the third earl (1578–1600), and his brother were implicated in the Gowrie Conspiracy to assassinate the king, but were themselves slain on the spot. If there were a conspiracy, however, it was of the king's own making, the hapless youths being set up. The earldom was forfeited and the very name of Ruthven outlawed. A cadet branch obtained the title Lord Ruthven in 1651 and from this descended Alexander Hore-Ruthven, Governor General of Australia, who was named first Earl of Gowrie in 1945.

ST. ANDREWS

Badge: St. Andrew and his saltire cross on
one side and a boar and oak tree on the
other, with the Latin motto *Dum spiro
spero* (While I breathe, I hope)
Gaelic: *Naomh Aindreas*

The small seaside town in Fife has an importance out
of all proportion to its size. St. Regulus had a vision
to take the relics of the Apostle Andrew to the ends
of the earth, and in 347 he landed on the Fife coast.
Around the shrine of St. Andrew, a cathedral was
built, which in the Middle Ages was the seat of an
archbishop. It was here, in 1411, that Scotland's first
university was established and the game of "gowf"
was played on the links. The Royal and Ancient Golf
Club was founded in 1754 and St. Andrews is now
the golfing capital of the world. The tartan, designed
in 1930, was intended for the Earl of St. Andrews, but
is now regarded as a district tartan.

ST. COLUMBA

Gaelic: *Columcille*

Born at Gartan, County Donegal, in 521, Colm was
a member of the prominent family of Ui Neill, who
entered the Celtic Church and founded the
monasteries of Derry in 548 and Durrow in 553. He
is said to have copied over 300 manuscripts in his
own hand, and it was an argument over the
copyright of one of these that triggered the dispute
that led him to depart from Ireland with twelve
disciples and settle on the first land they came to,
the island of Iona, in 563. From this base Columba
(Latin for "dove") set out to organize the Church in
Dalriada as well as convert the pagan Picts. After his
death in 597, Iona became the most sacred site in
Scotland and the burial place of many Scottish,
Norse, and Irish kings. This tartan was designed and
woven by Peter MacDonald in 1996 specifically to
raise money for the restoration of Iona Abbey.

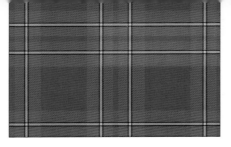

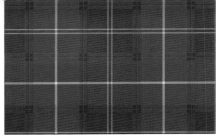

SALVATION ARMY

Badge: A fiery cross with the motto "Blood and fire"

In 1865 William Booth (1829–1912) founded the Christian Mission, which was renamed the Salvation Army in 1878. Its simple, practical version of evangelical Christianity spread throughout the world, while from the outset there was a strong policy of helping the homeless and the downtrodden in society. Important branches of its social work deal with women's problems and missing persons. This distinctive tartan was commissioned in 1983 by Captain H. Cooper to mark the centenary of the Perth Citadel and incorporates the Army's official colors: red (the blood of Christ), blue (the Heavenly Father), and yellow (the Pentecostal spirit). It is now worn by Salvationists all over Scotland.

SCOTLAND 2000

This is an interesting example of a commemorative tartan that can be worn by any Scot. It was commissioned in 1999 by the Strathmore Woollen Company to celebrate the millennium and has since been used as a trade tartan on a wide range of goods as well as plaids and kilts. Such commemorative tartans are a relatively new phenomenon and generally have a fairly short life span, but this attractive sett, based on the Scottish national colors and purple, traditionally associated with religious jubilees, seems destined to remain fashionable with tartan lovers.

SCOTT

Badge: A stag, with the Latin motto *Amo*
(I love)
Gaelic: *Scotach*

Uchtred Filius Scoti (Son of a Scot), who witnessed a charter of 1107, is regarded as the ancestor of this powerful Border clan whose main branches are the Scotts of Buccleuch and Balwearie. Sir Michael Scott of Balwearie, who died around 1300, was known as the "Wizard," as he was the leading scientist of his time. From the senior line came the Earls and, later, Dukes of Buccleuch. A branch of this, the Scotts of Harden, produced Sir Walter, the greatest of the early nineteenth-century novelists.

SCOTT (RED)

This tartan was designed in 1932 to mark the centenary of the death of the novelist Sir Walter Scott, who had played such a prominent part in the popular revival of tartan in the early nineteenth century. Ironically, Sir Walter was something of a purist who firmly believed that tartan in the true sense should be restricted to the Highland clans that had traditionally worn it, and argued that, at most, the Lowland families should only wear a check, similar to that worn by clergymen and shepherds, and this was what he himself preferred. He never wore the kilt itself, but had a plaid of this check. The Red Scott is now preferred to the traditional Scott tartan as a dress kilt.

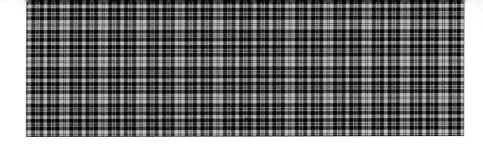

SCOTT, SIR WALTER

Badge: A nymph holding the sun and moon,
   with the Latin motto *Reparabit cornua*
   Phoebe (Phoebe will restore courage)

Most famous of all the Scotts, the poet and novelist was born in Edinburgh in 1771, descended from a minor branch of the family, the Scotts of Harden. He trained as a lawyer and became sheriff-deputy of Selkirkshire in 1799 and, later, clerk of sessions. His early literary reputation was as a poet, but he almost bankrupted himself in the purchase of his Abbotsford estate and turned increasingly to fiction to overcome his financial difficulties, notably in the Waverley novels first published in 1814. Facing ruin a second time in 1826, he redoubled his literary efforts in the last six years of his life. He was named baronet by George IV, but the title died with his son in 1847. His granddaughter Charlotte Lockhart married James Hope, who assumed the surname Hope-Scott. In 1874, their daughter Mary married Joseph Maxwell, son of Lord Herries, who assumed the name of Maxwell-Scott of Abbotsford.

SCOTTISH KNIGHTS TEMPLAR

The Poor Knights of Christ were a military order from their foundation in 1119 by Hugues des Payns and Godeffroi de St. Omer, knights from Burgundy and northern France, respectively, to protect pilgrims going to and from the Holy Land. They added the title Knights of the Temple of Solomon after moving to Jerusalem, and from this came the shorter name of Knights Templar, by which they are generally known. Eventually they had branches in most countries, and in Scotland the chapel of Rosslyn Castle was particularly associated with them. Although the original order was suppressed in 1314, they have been revived as a humanitarian body in more recent years. Three separate tartans were designed by Stuart Davidson of the Scottish Tartan Society for the Scottish Knights in 1998.

SCOTTISH PARLIAMENT

The Scottish Estates or Parliament had gradually evolved from the fourteenth century and latterly met in the Parliament House near St. Giles in Edinburgh. By the 1690s Scotland was increasingly governed, in fact if not in name, from Westminster, yet Scotland was not only a separate country but treated as an inferior by England. The barriers to Scottish commerce with the English colonies induced the disastrous Darien Scheme, whose collapse in 1700 provoked a strong Jacobite sentiment. It was realized that Scotland must either cut itself completely adrift from England or seek closer integration. The latter course was taken in 1707 and the Scottish Parliament ceased to exist. Agitation for its restoration surfaced from time to time throughout the nineteenth and early twentieth centuries, and although it failed to achieve the necessary majority in a referendum in 1979, it was overwhelmingly voted for in 1998, the year in which this tartan was created. It was officially adopted in 1999 following the opening of the Parliament.

SCRYMGEOUR

Badge: A mantled hand brandishing a saber,
with the Latin motto *Dissipate* (Scatter)

The badge and motto allude to the surname as an
ancient Scots word for "skirmisher" or "swordsman."
It arose from Sir Alexander Carron and his
descendants, who were hereditary standard-bearers
to the Kings of Scots from the early twelfth century. In
1298, Alexander the Schyrmeschur was appointed
Royal Standard-bearer and Constable of Dundee
Castle. His descendants acquired the lands of
Glassary, Argyll, in 1370. John Scrymgeour became
Viscount Dudhope in 1641, while John, the third
viscount, was elevated to Earl of Dundee at the
Restoration in 1660. His son was stripped of lands
and titles by the Duke of Lauderdale, whose brother
seized the estates, while the title went to John
Graham of Claverhouse ("Bonnie Dundee"). In 1953,
Henry Scrymgeour-Wedderburn regained the title.

SEMPILL

Badge: A stag's head, without a motto

It is alleged that this family was of Norman descent,
originating at St. Pol, but this has never been
proved. Certainly the family was established in
Renfrewshire by the late twelfth century, and in 1246
Robert de Sempill was named in a document of
Paisley Abbey. A few years later they had acquired
the hereditary office of Sheriff of Renfrew and in
1345 were confirmed in the lands of Elliotstoun in
that county. Sir Thomas Sempill died fighting for
James III at Sauchieburn (1488), while his son John,
first Lord Sempill (1489), was killed at Flodden
(1513). Robert, the third lord, was a staunch
supporter of Mary, Queen of Scots, but deserted her
at the end. Hugh, the twelfth lord, fought on the
Hanoverian side at Culloden and later commanded
the Black Watch. Best known of the family was the
soldier and poet Robert Sempill (c.1530–95).

SETON

Badge: A dragon breathing fire, with the
motto "Hazard, yet forward"

The name, meaning "sea town," alludes to Tranent on the southern shore of the Firth of Forth, nine miles east of Edinburgh, where Alexander Seton held lands as early as the middle of the twelfth century. Sir Christopher Seton married the sister of Robert the Bruce, but his adherence to the cause of independence led to a gory death. His brother, Sir Alexander, was governor of Berwick from 1327 to 1333 when that Border town was again briefly under Scottish rule, and only surrendered when the besieging English hanged his son and heir. In 1347, the Seton lands passed to Alan de Winton, who married Margaret Seton, and from them were descended the Lords Seton. Mary, sister of the fifth lord, was one of Queen Mary's Four Maries. Robert, the sixth lord, was named Earl of Winton in 1600. The actor Bruce Seton was the holder of the baronetcy of Abercorn that dated back to 1663.

SHAW

SIKH

Badge: A demi-lion holding a sword, with the Latin motto *Fide et fortitudine* (By faith and fortitude)

Gaelic: *Mac Ghille Sheathanaich*

One of the leading branches of Clan Chattan, the Shaws claim descent from Shaw, great-grandson of Angus, sixth chief of MacKintosh, who received the lands of Rothiemurchus for services rendered at the clan battle of the North Inch (1396). The clan lost its lands and was dispersed in 1595. The Shaws of Tordarroch, known as Clan Aidh, were likewise a branch of Clan Chattan. The Lowland Shaws were prominent in Ayrshire and Renfrewshire, their most famous clansman being Sir James Shaw from Kilmarnock, who became Lord Mayor of London.

Nothing illustrates more vividly the multiethnic nature of Scotland at the present time than the emergence of distinctive tartans for its Asian communities. The Sikhs were a religious sect that broke away from Brahmanical Hinduism around the same time that the Christian faith was rent asunder by the rise of Protestantism. It was founded by Nanak in the Punjab and derives its name from the Hindi word *sikha* (disciple). The holiest site is the Golden Temple at Amritsar, built by Ram Das in 1579. The first Sikhs to settle in Scotland arrived just after World War II and it was to celebrate the fiftieth anniversary of his family's arrival in Scotland that A. J. Singh commissioned the tartan by Kinloch Anderson in 1999.

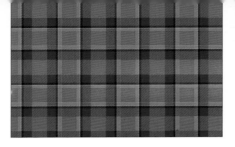 

SINCLAIR

SINGH

Badge: A cock, with the motto "Commit thy
work to God"
Gaelic: *Mac na Ceardadh*

This northern clan traces its origins to St. Clair in
Normandy. William de St. Clair came with the
Conqueror, while his grandson obtained the barony
of Roslin from David I. Sir Henry supported the
Bruce, and his son Sir William died with the Black
Douglas in Spain. Henry Sinclair was named Earl of
Orkney in 1379, while his grandson also became
Earl of Caithness. Sir John Sinclair of Ulbster
(1754–1835) was both an improving landowner
and prolific poet, as well as a pioneer of
demography and compiler of the first Statistical
Account of Scotland.

The tenth and last guru was Govind Rai
(1675–1708), who took the affix Singh (lion) in lieu
of Rai and remodeled the Sikh organization, which
he named *Khalsa* (pure). A separate Singh tartan
was likewise commissioned in 1999, partly to
celebrate the tercentenary of the Khalsa order
and partly for the use of Sikhs with the surname
of Singh. This tartan was manufactured by
Lochcarron at the behest of Sirdar Iqbal Singh, the
Sikh businessman who translated Burns into Urdu
and is the Laird of Birkwood Castle, Lesmahagow.
In the tradition of Raeburn's famous portrait of the
MacDonnell of Glengarry, a painting entitled *Laird
Singhs His Tartan Praises* by Rabindra and Amrit
Kaur Singh was displayed in an exhibition at the
Royal Museum of Scotland in 2001.

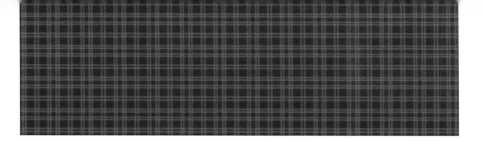

SKENE

Badge: An arm issuing from a cloud and
holding a laurel crown, with the Latin
motto *Virtutis regia merces* (A palace is
the reward of valor)

Gaelic: *MacSgian*

According to William Skene, the Celtic historian, the clan was founded by Struan Robertson, who saved the king's life by slaying a wolf with his knife (*sgian*) and was rewarded with the lands of Skene in Aberdeenshire. John de Skene appears in the Ragman Rolls (1296) and his grandson Robert, a supporter of Bruce, received a baronial charter from the king. When the direct line died out in 1827, the chiefship passed to James, fourth Earl of Fife, a nephew of the last chief. The most famous clansman was William F. Skene (1809–92), a prolific writer on Celtic Scotland who became Historiographer Royal for Scotland in 1881.

SPENS

Badge: A stag's head, with the Latin motto
Si deus quis contra? (If God is present,
who is against?)

This surname originated from an official in royal and noble households, the dispenser or keeper of the larder, which gave rise to such English names as Dispenser, Spenser, and Spencer. These names also occur in Scotland, but there are also the distinctly Scottish variants of Spens and Spence (from the Scots word for a store-room or, more vaguely, any small living room or bedroom). It appears in Scottish legal documents in the Latin forms Dispensator or Dispensa from the late twelfth century. Henry de Spens of Lathallan in Fife (died 1300) claimed descent from the Thanes of Fife. His descendant Sir Patrick Spens accompanied Princess Margaret to Norway, and his death in 1281 is the subject of one of Scotland's best-known ballads. Patrick Spens, who served in the Garde Ecossaise (the French royal bodyguard), founded the French family of Spens d'Estignols de Lassere in the fifteenth century. His namesake, Sir Patrick Spense (1885–1973), became first Lord Spens of Blairsanquhar, Fife, in 1959.

STEWART OF APPIN

Badge: The head of a unicorn, with the Scots motto *Quhidder will zie?* (Whither will ye?)

Gaelic: *Stiubhart*

The large and powerful Clan Stewart (or Stuart) traces its origins back to Walter, sixth High Steward of Scotland, who married Marjorie Bruce, daughter of Robert I, and thus founded the dynasty that ruled Scotland ever since (and whose descendants continue to occupy the throne of the United Kingdom to this day). The Stewarts of Appin claim descent from Dougal Stewart, son of Sir John Stewart of Lorn, who was murdered in 1463. After this calamity, Dougal fled into the remote Appin district to escape his father's enemies. His son Duncan became chamberlain to James IV. The Appin Stewarts were staunch supporters of Montrose during the religious wars and fought with distinction at Inverlochy, Auldern, and Kilsyth. They later adhered to the Jacobite cause and fought at Killiecrankie (1689), Sheriffmuir (1715), and Culloden (1746), inevitably suffering the consequences of being on the losing side.

STEWART OF ATHOLL

Badge: The head of a unicorn, with the Scots motto *Quhidder will zie?* (Whither will ye?)

Gaelic: *Stiubhart*

Alexander Stewart (1343–1405), the fourth legitimate son of Robert II and thus a great-grandson of the Bruce, bore the title of Earl of Buchan, but unofficially he was feared as the Wolf of Badenoch. One of the most colorful characters in Scotland's turbulent history, he sired numerous illegitimate sons, from whom descended the Stewarts of Aberdenshire, Banffshire, and Moray, as well as the powerful Stewart Earls of Atholl. One of his sons was the progenitor of the Atholl Stewarts who, in 1437, married the widow of James I, murdered only a few weeks previously. The assassins were swiftly apprehended and cruelly put to death. The chief plotter was the elderly Earl of Atholl, whose estates were forfeited and passed to the widow's new husband, Sir James Stewart, younger of Invermeath, known as the Black Knight of Lorn. Their son, Sir John Stewart of Balveny, was named Earl of Atholl by his half brother, James II.

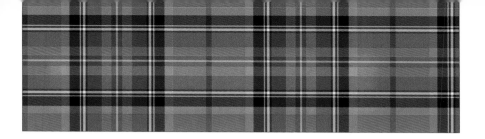

STEWART OF GALLOWAY

Badge: A pelican feeding her young with her own blood, and the Latin motto *Virescit vulnere virtus* (Courage gains strength from a wound)

Gaelic: *Stiubhart*

The Stewarts of Galloway, rather than the royal Stewarts, are regarded as the premier line because of their direct descent from Sir John Stewart of Bonkyl (now Buncle or Bonkhill in Berwickshire), the second son of Alexander, fourth High Steward of Scotland, and great-uncle of the Steward who married Marjorie Bruce. The good Sir John was killed at the battle of Stirling Bridge in 1297. The Stewart of Galloway was raised to the peerage in 1607 with the title of Lord Garlies, and his descendant became Baron Stewart of Garlies in the United Kingdom peerage in 1796. The Scottish earldom of Galloway, however, was founded in 1623, reviving a title that had been held by ancestors of Robert the Bruce through his Celtic mother, Marjorie of Galloway. The Earls of Galloway have also served as lords lieutenant of the county that alludes to their surname, the Stewartry of Kirkcudbright.

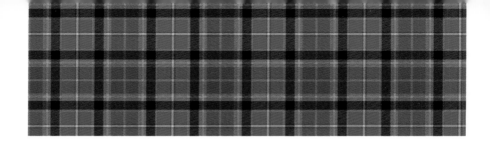

STIRLING AND BANNOCKBURN

Badge: A saltire cross with a lion rampant at the center and two caltraps and two spur rowels in the angles

Gaelic: *Struighli*

In the Middle Ages, Stirling was one of the most important places strategically, for whoever possessed its castle controlled communications between the north and south of Scotland. Occupation of this stronghold was vital in the Wars of Independence, and it is associated with two of the greatest victories against the English, won by William Wallace at Stirling Bridge (1297) and by Robert the Bruce at Bannockburn (1314).

Bannockburn, on the outskirts of Stirling, was the home of the great Wilson's tartan manufactory, which began weaving the distinctive check cloth around 1790, mainly for the Scottish regiments. It was also very active in the promotion of the tartan fashion from the 1820s onward. This district tartan was devised by Wilson's in 1847 for the local Caledonian Society.

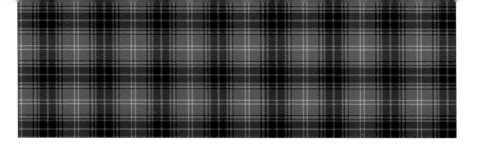

STONE OF DESTINY

Tradition maintains that the Stone of Destiny was the very stone that Jacob used as a pillow when he dreamed of angels ascending into heaven. Taken to Ireland by the Celts as they migrated across Europe, it became Lia Fail, the sacred stone on which the kings of Ireland were crowned at Tara. The Scots brought it with them when they crossed over to Dalriada, and it was probably used for coronations at Iona or Dunstaffnage before reaching its final resting place at Scone. It was seized by Edward I in 1296 and taken off to London. By the Treaty of Northampton (1328) it should have been returned to Scotland, but this piece of bad faith was not remedied until exactly 700 years after it was stolen, when Prime Minister John Major removed it from Westminster Abbey and sent it to Edinburgh, where it is now on view in the castle. This tartan was produced for MacNaughtons of Pitlochry to celebrate the Stone's repatriation.

STUART, CHARLES EDWARD

A pair of trews, preserved in the West Highland Museum at Fort William and believed to have been worn by the Young Pretender at the Battle of Culloden in April 1746, is the basis of this colorful tartan. Prince Charles Edward Louis Philip Casimir Stuart (or Stewart) was born in Rome in 1720, the elder son of Prince James Stuart (the Old Pretender). In 1744, he went to France to head a proposed invasion of Britain; although this project was aborted, he landed at Eriskay in July 1745 with seven companions and raised the Jacobite standard at Glenfinnan soon afterward. The Highland clans rallied to his banner, swept all before them, and got as far as Derby before the tide turned. A series of reverses culminated in the decisive defeat at Culloden. On the run for five months, Bonnie Prince Charlie was helped by Flora MacDonald to escape into exile in France and Italy, where he eventually died in 1788.

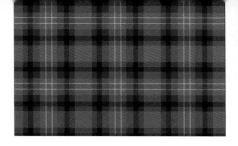

STURROCK

SUTHERLAND

It seems probable that the origin of this surname was occupational, meaning "cow herd" or "stock master." It first appears in Angus in the middle of the fifteenth century, when Laurence Sturrock, chaplain in Aberdeen, witnessed a document of 1448. Five years later he was recorded as the vicar of Colvill in Angus. Later bearers of this surname, however, took a prominent part in the religious wars of the seventeenth century and were ranked among the Covenanters and dissenters of the period. Most famous of this clan is Peter Sturrock, who held office as Provost of Kilmarnock for twelve years and was subsequently a member of parliament for that burgh. He is best remembered as the founder of the worldwide Burns Federation and its first president (1885–99).

Badge: A cat, with the French motto *Sans peur* (Without fear)

Gaelic: *Suthurlarach*

The premier earldom of the British Isles was conferred in 1228 on William, Lord of Sutherland, great-grandson of Freskin de Moravia, ancestor of the Murrays. Support for the crown was reinforced by the marriage of the fourth earl to a daughter of Robert Bruce. The earldom passed to the Gordons of Aboyne when the ninth earl died without issue. From this warlike clan, perennially feuding with their Gunn and Mackay neighbors, was raised the Sutherland Highlanders, or Ninety-third Foot, in 1800, best remembered as the "Thin Red Line" at Balaclava in the Crimean War.

TARTAN ARMY

The term "Tartan Army" was coined by a sports journalist in the mid-1970s to describe the supporters of Scottish soccer teams playing abroad, on account of the fact that they were invariably clad in kilts, a feature that made them instantly recognizable. In the ensuing decades they came to be identified with good-natured bonhomie and a natural ability to get on with supporters of rival national teams and the people of the host countries. As a tribute to the Tartan Army, regarded as Scotland's goodwill ambassadors, Keith Lumsden of the Scottish Tartans Society designed this sett in time for the 1998 Soccer World Cup. It blends the Royal Stewart and Black Watch (two of the most popular tartans worn by fans), and since then has been worn by Scottish supporters of international sporting events in general.

TAYLOR

Badge: A clutch of five arrows, with the Gaelic motto *Aonibh ri cheile* (All together as one)

Gaelic: *Taillear*

This is another occupational surname that occurs frequently all over Scotland in various guises, including Tailor and Taillyeur. Alexander le Taillur was the first of this name on record, having been appointed valet to Alexander III in 1276. In the siege of Dunbar Castle in 1296, Brice le Taillur was listed as one of those who was captured by the English. At least half a dozen gentlemen of this surname signed the Ragman Rolls in the same year. It should be noted that the Latin term for a tailor was *cissor*, and there are also numerous references to people surnamed Cissor or Scissor in the fourteenth and fifteenth centuries. Traditionally, Taylors are regarded as a sept of Clan Cameron, because one of its progenitors was a shadowy figure known as the Black Tailor of the Battle-ax *(Taillear dubh na tuaighe)*. Consequently, this modern tartan features the Cameron colors.

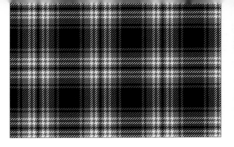

TWEEDSIDE

This district tartan, first recorded by Wilson's of Bannockburn around 1840, was designed at a time when Highland myth and romance were spreading through the Lowlands and Borders. It takes its name from the river that, rising in southern Lanarkshire, traverses the ancient counties of Peebles and Selkirk and enters the North Sea at Berwick, which until 1482 was a Scottish town. For only part of its course, therefore, the Tweed marks the frontier between Scotland and England. It is not only one of Scotland's finest salmon rivers but a stream with profuse historic connections. The Tweed was the inspiration of James Hogg and Sir Walter Scott and was frequently apostrophized in their poetry and fiction.

URQUHART

Badge: A demi-otter, with the Latin motto
Per mare per terras (By sea and land)
Gaelic: *Urchurdan*

Originally a branch of Clan Forbes, the Urquharts take their name from the glen and castle near Loch Ness. Early in the fourteenth century, William Urquhart became hereditary Sheriff of Cromarty and by marriage acquired lands in that district. Sir Thomas Urquhart, translator of Rabelais, fought on the Royalist side in the Civil War but died in 1660 on hearing the news of the Restoration. He also compiled a clan genealogy, showing himself as 143rd in direct descent from Adam and Eve.

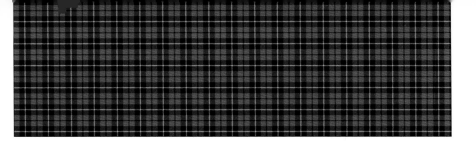

WALLACE

Badge: An armored right arm holding a
sword, with the Latin motto *Pro libertate
sperandum est* (For liberty we must hope)

Gaelic: *Uallas*

To prove how ancient this clan is, early historians claimed descent from the Volcae of northern Gaul, but in fact the name merely described someone of Welsh (i.e., Strathclyde Briton) origin. The clan is descended from Richard Wallace, who held lands in Ayrshire (Riccarton is derived from Richard's toun). His son Malcolm held the estate of Ellerslie near Kilmarnock, where his younger son William was born around 1270, not Elderslie near Paisley (a late eighteenth-century invention). From the Wallaces of Ayrshire came the family of Craigie; Frances Wallace, later Mrs. Dunlop of Dunlop, was the "mother confessor" of Robert Burns. Other famous clansmen include General Lew Wallace, author of *Ben Hur*; the Pacific explorer Samuel Wallis; Poland's Solidarity leader Lech Walesa; and the late Duchess of Windsor (born Bessie Wallis Warfield).

WEIR

Badge: A boar on a cap of maintenance,
   with the Latin motto *Vero nihil verius*
   (Nothing is truer than the truth)

The family motto is a fine example of a Latin pun, alluding to the original form of the surname, which stems from the Norman town of Vere. A knight from that district doubtless accompanied the Conqueror and it was his descendants who migrated to Scotland early in the eleventh century, acquiring lands around Lesmahagow and Blackwood in Lanarkshire. Radulphus de Ver was among the Scottish knights captured with William the Lyon at the siege of Alnwick in 1174. Major Thomas Weir of Carluke was burned at the stake in 1670 for bestiality, incest, and witchraft, his sister being hanged for the same offenses. A generation later, the Weirs of Lesmahagow were prominent among the Covenanters who fought at Drumclog and Bothwell Brig. Most famous of the family include the industrialist and statesman William Weir (1877–1950), first Viscount Weir of Cathcart, a direct descendant of Robert Burns; the shipowner Andrew Weir, first Lord Inverforth (1919); Robert Weir, who wrote "O Canada" (the Canadian national anthem); and the Australian-born film director Peter Weir.

WEMYSS

Badge: A swan, with the French motto
Je pense (I think)

Gaelic: *Uaimh* (Cave or den)

This Fife place-name is believed to allude to the caves along the north shore of the Firth of Forth. Wemyss (pronounced "Weems") Castle was a stronghold of an ancient family of Celtic origin, related to the MacDuff thanes of Fife, a younger son of which obtained the lands of Wemyss around 1160. Sir Michael de Wemyss was among the courtiers tasked with bringing the Maid of Norway to Scotland, but a few years later signed the Ragman Rolls in 1296. Later he fought under Robert the Bruce, for which the English destroyed his castle as a reprisal. His descendant Sir David de Wemyss was slain at Flodden (1513). Sir John Wemyss was one of the first baronets of Nova Scotia (1625), later first Lord Wemyss (1628) and Earl of Wemyss (1633). Lord Elcho, elder son of the fifth earl, fought at Culloden and was convicted of treason. The estates and earldom passed to his brother, the ancestor of the present Earl of Wemyss and March, whereas the clan chiefship passed to the third son, James Wemyss of Wemyss.

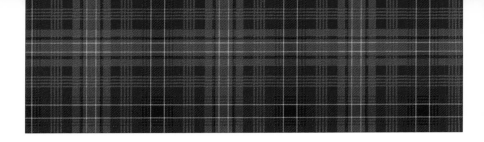

WILSON

Badge: A demi-lion rampant, with the Latin
motto *Semper vigilans* (Ever watchful)

The patronymic, son of Will or William, is widespread throughout Scotland and first appears in documents in the middle of the fifteenth century, although traditionally the Wilsons (or Willsons) are regarded as septs of the Gunn and MacInnes clans through Wilson ancestors who had close associations with them. The Bannockburn weaver William Wilson had a monopoly of tartan manufacture for the Scottish regiments from about 1765 and this particular tartan, woven in 1780 to celebrate the wedding of his son William to Janet Paterson, is one of the oldest of the family tartans. Three later variants of it are recorded by the Scottish Tartans Society. Famous Wilsons include Alexander Wilson (1766–1813), the Paisley-born father of American ornithology, and John Wilson of Kilmarnock, who printed and published the first edition of Robert Burns's poetry in 1786. The Wilsons nicknamed "Electric Charlie" (1886–1972) and "Engine Charlie" (1890–1961) were bosses of General Electric and General Motors, respectively, and long-term cabinet members or advisers to the U.S. government. Woodrow Wilson, the twenty-eighth president of the United States, was of Covenanting descent.

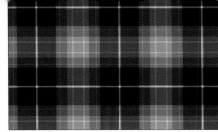

WITHERSPOON

The derivation of this curious name appears to be pastoral, from *wedder* (sheep) and *spong* (pasture). It occurs in many parts of England in various forms, reflecting the importance of sheep rearing and the woolen industry from the Middle Ages onward. It is also recorded in southern Scotland in the thirteenth century when Roger Wytthispon witnessed a charter in Renfrewshire, while a Widderspune served as fowler to James V. Best known of this surname was Reverend John Witherspoon (1723–94), who went to America in 1768 to become principal of the college that is now Princeton University and who was the only clergyman to sign the Declaration of Independence.

WRENS

The Women's Royal Naval Service (WRNS) was founded in 1917. Women were enrolled in many clerical and administrative duties at naval bases and other establishments in order to free men for combat duties. Dame Katherine Furse (1875–1952) was its first director. The service was disbanded in 1919 but reactivated in 1939 and considerably expanded and retained as a permanent fixture. The motto "Never at Sea" lost its literal meaning in the 1980s as the personnel of the WRNS began undertaking seagoing duties. From the outset, members of the service were popularly known as "Wrens" and it was for the Scottish ladies of the Wrens Association that this tartan, with its distinctive navy blue ground, was produced by D. C. Dalgleish in 1997 to celebrate the eightieth anniversary of the service.

IRISH TARTANS

Introduction

Although the peasantry of Ireland, like their kinsmen in Scotland and the Isle of Man, wore a woolen plaid that was folded and belted in such a way as to form a covering for the upper part of the body as well as a kilt for the lower part, the distinctive checkered cloth that gradually evolved as tartan was not employed, certainly not in the way it developed in the Highlands and Islands of Scotland, either as a district tartan or a clan tartan. Cloth was sometimes woven with a slight check of contrasting threads, but nothing so distinctive as a tartan emerged, and the cloth used for Irish kilts tended to be a relatively plain color, in shades or brown, saffron yellow, or green.

There was no identification of individual families or clans by tartan, as in Scotland, and no need to regard it as a threat to (English) law and order, which led to the outlawing of tartan in eighteenth-century Scotland. Nor, by the same token, was there the extraordinary resurgence of checkered cloth in Ireland that accompanied the Romantic movement in early nineteenth-century Scotland. Nevertheless, tartan cloth, in fabrics of all kinds, enjoyed a measure of popularity in Ireland (as, indeed, everywhere else) in the late nineteenth century, but it would be impossible to attach much significance to it, as it merely reflected a prevailing fashion, notably in women's dress. Menswear, in the form of plaids and kilts in the Scottish style, died out in Ireland in the seventeenth and early eighteenth centuries, and thereafter was confined to the pipe bands of the Irish regiments, who wore plain saffron or green kilts.

Nevertheless, it was inevitable that the enthusiasm for tartan associated with clans and families

Left: Pipers in a St. Patrick's Day parade

Above: Drummer in a St. Patrick's Day parade

in Scotland should not spill over into Ireland. This much is evident in a book entitled *Clan Originaux*, which was published by Claude Brothers and Company of Paris in 1880. This curious work is an extremely rare book, and the only copy now believed to be extant was discovered in the United States recently and is now in the possession of Pendleton Mills in Portland, Oregon. It is, in fact, virtually the only source of information regarding distinctive Irish tartans in the nineteenth century. In Irish as well as Scottish Gaelic, *breacan* is the term used indiscriminately for checkered cloth as well as tartan; significantly, in Irish, the word has the secondary meaning of clouts (rags) or old clothes.

There are relatively few Irish tartans that can be regarded as clan or family tartans in the Scottish sense. They include O'Brien, Clan Cian (O'Carroll), O'Connor, Duffy, O'Farrell, Fitzgerald, Fitzpatrick, Forde, MacGuire, Murphy, and O'Neill.

Most, if not all of these, were featured in *Clan Originaux*, but their antecedents are shrouded in mystery. Some at least have turned out to be variants of Scottish tartans.

The vast majority of Irish tartans, described in this book, are of very recent origin. Most of them were, in fact, created in the 1990s by MacNaughtons of Pitlochry and their subsidiary, House of Edgar (Woollens) Limited of Perth, primarily for the people of Irish descent who constitute a large proportion of the population of Scotland, arising out of the migrations from the 1840s onward. And if the Scots came from Ulster in the first place, back in the fifth and sixth centuries, it should be remembered that the Ulster Scots, from whom so many Americans (including at least sixteen presidents) are descended, were Lowland Scots who were "planted" in Ireland by King James VI in the early seventeenth century. The Scots and the Irish have a common language and culture going back thousands of years, so the extension of Scottish tartan to Ireland is merely the latest manifestation of the links that bind the two nations.

The modern tartans represent the thirty-two counties and four historic provinces of Ireland. For convenience, two representative tartans from the Isle of Man are included here, the third of the Goidelic (Q-Celtic) countries whose history is inextricably linked with Ireland through its Hiberno-Norse heritage.

ANTRIM

Badge: A red lion rampant on a gold field,
   surmounted by a red hand flanked by
   towers
Gaelic: *Aontroim*

One of the six counties of Northern Ireland, Antrim is geographically and politically the closest to Scotland. The Romans never landed in Ireland but it was to Antrim that the Romano-British boy Patricius (Padruig or Patrick) was brought as a slave before converting the Irish to Christianity. It was from here that the Scots set out to conquer Dalriada in the fifth century and from whence Columba and his followers embarked on their evangelical mission to Iona in 563. It was the last part of Ireland to fall to the English in the twelfth century and was briefly under the rule of Edward Bruce, brother of King Robert, in 1315. In Tudor times there was a sustained immigration of Lowland Scots into Antrim.

ARMAGH

Badge: A gold Irish harp on a green field
Gaelic: *Ard Mhacha* (Heights of the goddess
   Macha)

This inland county of Northern Ireland derives its name from Eamhain Mhacha, a Celtic stronghold erected around 300 B.C., and located near the modern city of Armagh. From its imposing appearance, it was supposed that this was the capital of Ulster in ancient times. For this reason, St. Patrick deliberately chose it as the location of the Christian faith. From then on it was the ecclesiastical capital of Ireland, and its archbishop recognized as the primate of all Ireland from the eighth century to this day. Apart from its strong religious associations, Armagh was for many centuries the center of the Irish fruit-growing and flax industries. The predominant green and brown colors of the tartan reflect the Armagh countryside.

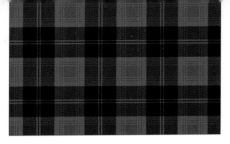

CARLOW

Badge: Dimidiated lions rampant and
  couchant
Gaelic: *Ceatharlach* (Four lakes)

This name was given to a town and its surrounding
county, the second-smallest in all Ireland, founded
at the beginning of the thirteenth century by King
John. He granted it to William, Earl of Pembroke,
who built its impressive Norman castle. It is an
inland county of Leinster, bounded by Kildare and
Wicklow on the north, Wicklow and Wexford on the
east, and Laois and Kilkeny on the west. Apart from
its Norman associations, Carlow is renowned for its
dolmens, prehistoric standing stones, of which
Mount Browne, northeast of the town, is the largest
in Ireland. Carlow was sacked by Rory Oge O'More
in Tudor times and played a prominent role in the
Rising of 1798.

CAVAN

Badge: Two gold balls on a blue field with a
  Crusader tent above and a green lion
  rampant below
Gaelic: *An Cabhán* (The hollow)

One of the three historic counties of Ulster that lie
within the Republic of Ireland, Cavan is a mainly
agricultural area, noted for rugged mountains in the
north and its numerous lakes. The River Shannon
has its source here. When the Anglo-Norman
occupation began in the twelfth century, the area was
controlled by the O'Rourkes and O'Reillys. It retained
a rugged independence until the seventeenth century
when it was systematically "planted" by James VI
and I, which accounts for the many Lowland Scottish
names in the area. It was also the home of the
Sheridan family, from which came the playwright
Richard Sheridan and the ancestors of Philip
Sheridan, a general in the American Civil War.

CLODAGH

Gaelic: *Clodagh*

In recent times this is a popular girl's name and refers to an ancient region of Ireland that derives its name from a river in County Cork and a small village of the same name, but how it came to be applied to a tartan is something of a mystery. The Scottish Tartans Society records that a bagpipe manufacturer in Northern Ireland (1979) stated that "it has been established that it originated somewhere in the Bog of Allen in Southern Ireland," but no date was suggested and this wetland is nowhere near Clodagh. In fact, this tartan bears a close resemblance to the King George VI tartan (a variant of the Royal Stewart), with more than a hint of the MacBeth tartan for good measure.

CONNAUGHT

Badge: Dimidiated spread eagle and an arm brandishing a sword
Gaelic: *Connachta* (The land of Conn)

The northwestern province of Ireland was a *firbolg* (state) in pre-Celtic times. Around 150 it came under a Gaelic dynasty tracing its origins to Conn of the Hundred Battles, with its capital at Croghan in County Roscommon. It spread across the Shannon and moved its capital to Tara around 250. Connaught continued as a separate kingdom until 1224, and its ruler, Turlough O'Connor, became High King of Ireland in 1119. Henry III granted Connaught to Richard de Burgh. The last of this line married Lionel, Duke of Clarence, and Connaught became an English royal title, last borne by Prince Arthur, third son of Queen Victoria (1850–1942). There are three tartans: the one here or with additional white and red stripes, produced by Lochcarron in 1993.

CONROY

Badge: An open Bible on a blue ground with
a castellated band of gold at the top
Gaelic: *Ui Maol Chonn Ruaidh* (The family of
the servant of Red Conn)

This is a rare example of an Irish family tartan. The
name implies that its progenitor was the servant or
devotee of a holy man, the epithet *maol* (which in
modern Irish means "bald") signifying a person who
had taken the tonsure of monasticism. The first and
foremost of this clan was Torna O'Mulconry, who
flourished in the first half of the fourteenth century
and won a celebrated bardic contest. Several
generations of this family were hereditary bards to
the O'Connor kings. Fearfassa O'Mulconry was
one of the chroniclers of the celebrated *Annals of
the Four Masters.* By contrast, the tartan itself
was commissioned by L. B. Conroy of Sydney,
New South Wales, in 1986.

CORK

Badge: Two towers bearing the Cross of
St. Patrick, flanking a sailing ship
Gaelic: *Corcaigh*

This tartan was designed for MacNaughtons of
Pitlochry by Polly Wittering of the House of Edgar.
Cork is the largest of the Irish counties, forming part
of the ancient province of Munster. It takes its name
from its capital city, founded by St. Finbarr in the
seventh century, and the Protestant cathedral stands
on the site of his original foundation. The Norsemen
sacked the town in 821 but it was an important
Danish stronghold for two centuries. It submitted to
Henry II in 1172 and was thereafter under English
control. It played a major role in the Civil War (1922–
23), when it was controlled by the Irish Republican
Army until they were driven out by the National Army
under Michael Collins. Collins was ambushed and
killed at Beal na mBlath soon afterward.

DONEGAL

Badge: A red cross-crosslet on a white shield set within wavy bands of green and gold

Gaelic: *Dún na nGall* (Stronghold of the foreigner)

Gall is a word that alludes to the fact that the town was fortified by the Norsemen, and the county on the extreme northwest coast of Ireland derived its name from the town, superseding the much older name of Tir Chonaill (Conall country). As this name suggests, its native dynasty was founded by Conal Gulban, a son of the legendary Niall of the Nine Hostages. County Donegal gives the lie to the expression "Southern Ireland" as a synonym for the Irish Republic, because it is actually the most northerly of the thirty-two counties. The district tartan, created by the House of Edgar in 1996, represents the Atlantic Ocean as well as the green countryside.

DOWN

Badge: Three wheat sheaves, a fish, and a ship at sea

Gaelic: *Dún* (Stronghold)

The most easterly county of Ireland, it derives its name from Dún Pádraig, the stronghold of St. Patrick, on which the modern county town of Downpatrick now stands. Nearby are the ruins of Saul Abbey (*sabhall* meaning "barn"), an Augustinian friary erected on the site of Patrick's first church. The early history of Down is shrouded in mystery, although the county abounds in cromlechs, standing stones, and chambered cairns, testifying to occupation thousands of years ago. It was also the first part of Ireland to be settled by the Anglo-Normans. Dundrum Castle, built by the De Courcy family, is a reminder of their former power.

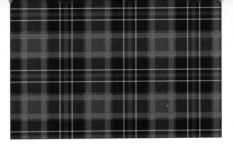

DOYLE

Badge: Three red stags' heads
Gaelic: *Dubh gall* (Dark foreigner)

This is a prime example of an Irish clan tartan that is not only of very recent origin (1999), but whose use is very strictly controlled, as it may only be worn by persons of this surname who have enrolled with the Clan Doyle Society, based in Dromana, Victoria, Australia. The surname is derived from the old Irish term used to describe Vikings of Danish origin, as opposed to the blond Vikings from western Norway (*fionn gall*, "fair-haired foreigner"). From these terms come the anglicized names Doyle or Dougal and Fingal. Variants of the surname include MacDougal, MacDowell, and MacDoual. Famous members of the clan include the caricaturist John Doyle and his son, the painter Richard Doyle, as well as the surgeon and novelist Sir Arthur Conan Doyle.

DUBLIN

Badge: A raven perched on a hurdle
Gaelic: *Dubh Linn* (Black pool)

The preferred Gaelic name for the Irish capital is Baile Atha Cliath (Town at the ford of the hurdles), although the name anglicized as Dublin was certainly in use by 291, the year in which the men of Dublin defeated the people of Leinster. Although Patrick established a church in Dublin around 450, the place was of little importance until 832, when the Viking leader Thorkel I made it the capital of the Hiberno-Norse kingdom. The Danes were driven out by the Normans in 1171 and it became the center of English power in Ireland. Invaded by the Scots in 1315 and Cromwell in 1649 and the scene of numerous insurrections from 1534 until 1916, Dublin was also badly damaged in 1922 when Nationalist artillery shelled the Four Courts, a stronghold of the IRA. The modern city retains much of its Georgian splendor.

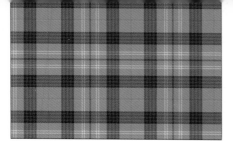

FERMANAGH

Badge: A castle flying the Cross of St. Patrick
over stylized blue and white waves
Gaelic: *Fear Manach* or *Fearmach Eanach*
(Country of the lakes)

The ancient name for this Ulster county alludes to the profusion of lakes, notably Lough Erne, which bisects it, although some scholars argue for a derivation from Fir Monach, a tribe that settled in the area in the third century. Such place-names as Clankelly and Clanawley refer to some of the oldest families in the district, although it was also the home of the ancient Guarii, from whom descend the Maguires, whose name, in turn, comes from *mach uire* (people of the waters). It is not surprising that a pale blue ground should have been adopted for the county tartan. The area abounds in ancient tumuli and Danish raths, monastic settlements, and Anglo-Norman castles, a microcosm of Ireland's turbulent history.

FITZGERALD

Badge: The red saltire Cross of St. Patrick
on a plain white ground

This is one of five Fitzgerald tartans, dating from around 1900 when Colonel Fitzgerald, commander of the Baluchi regiment in the Indian Army, devised a tartan worn by the pipers of the regimental band. *Fitz* is the Anglo-Norman version of the French word *fils* (son). This family traces its descent from Walter, Son of Other, castellan of Windsor at the time of the Domesday Book (1086). One of his younger sons, Gerald, became constable of Pembroke Castle and married Nesta, sister of Griffith, King of South Wales. In 1169 their third son, Maurice, was recruited by Dermot, King of Ireland, as a mercenary and was rewarded with lands in Wexford. He spearheaded the Anglo-Norman invasion of 1170. Many of the Fitzgeralds held high office and from them came the Earls of Kildare and Desmond.

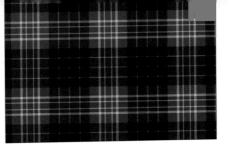

FITZPATRICK

Badge: Three gold fleur-de-lys over the
Cross of St. Andrew
Gaelic: *Mac Giolla Phádraig* (Son of the
servant of St. Patrick)

This is an interesting example of the rendering of an ancient Irish name in the Anglo-Norman idiom. Other anglicized variants include Gilpatrick and Kilpatrick. This clan traces its origins back to Eremon, legendary ruler of the Milesians, although the earliest verifiable ancestor was Giolla Phádraig, Lord of Upper Ossory in the tenth century. There are still many people with this surname in the Kilkenny district, although it is also commonly found in Britain, North America, and Australia, reflecting the extent of the Irish diaspora since the late seventeenth century. The tartan shown here is a modern variant of one recorded in *Clan Originaux* (1880), with a green ground in place of the original gray.

GALWAY

Badge: A gold lion rampant in a blue shield
superimposed on a medieval sailing ship
Gaelic: *Gaillimh*

This county in the province of Connaught in the west of Ireland is second in size (after Cork) and noted for the rich variety of its coastal and inland scenery. The rugged Atlantic coast is deeply indented and studded with islands, while the interior is dominated by the bogs of Connemara and numerous lakes, of which Lough Corrib is the largest, while the Shannon forms the southern boundary of the county. Ancient cromlechs and tumuli, Viking settlements, and Anglo-Norman abbeys and castles testify to the long history of the district. Tuam Castle was built in 1161 by Roderick O'Connor, King of Ireland, shortly before the Anglo-Norman invasion. In 1919 Clifden was the landfall of Alcock and Brown, the first men to fly the Atlantic.

IRISH NATIONAL

Badge: A gold harp in the form of a winged
   female, on a blue ground, and the Gaelic
   motto *Erin gu bragh* (Ireland forever)
Gaelic: *Éire* (The popular form *Erin* is actually
   derived from the dative case *Éirinn*)

This tartan was suggested by Jo Nisbet of Pipers
Cove, New Jersey, and designed by Polly Wittering
of the House of Edgar in Perth for MacNaughtons
of Pitlochry—a fine example of American and
Scottish cooperation in the service of the millions of
expatriate or hyphenated Irishmen the world over.
With a range of county and district tartans as well
as several family tartans in the past decade, there
can be few people of Irish descent who would not
qualify for one of these, but in default of a county
sett this is a universal tartan whose colors
symbolize Christianity (gold and white) as well as
the Emerald Isle.

KILDARE

Badge: A serpent on a white ground
Gaelic: *Cill Dara* (Church of the oak)

The name of this county in the ancient province of
Leinster is derived from the oak tree in whose
shade St. Brigid constructed her cell. The daughter
of an Ulster prince, Brigid (453–523) took the veil at
the age of fourteen and founded four convents, of
which the one in Kildare was the most important.
She ranks after Patrick and Columba as the
greatest of the Irish saints and, as St. Bride, was
also widely revered in Scotland. Kildare is a county
with numerous monastic remains and Anglo-
Norman castles. The sparsely populated inland
area includes the large tract known as the Bog of
Allen, home of the legendary warrior Finn MacCool
(Fionn Mac Cumhaill). Near the town of Kildare is
the Curragh, once the main base in Ireland of the
British Army.

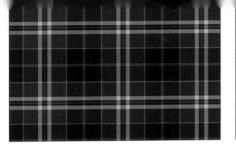

KILKENNY

Badge: Dimidiated arms showing three
wheat sheaves and three angular knots
Gaelic: *Cill Chainnigh* (Church of St. Canice)

Canice (or Kenneth) was a contemporary and
disciple of Columba, undertaking missions to the
Picts and Scots before returning to Ireland and
founding a monastery, the site of which is now
occupied by the cathedral that bears his name,
erected in 1255. The county was founded by King
John in the early thirteenth century, replacing the
ancient kingdom of Ossory (Osraige). The district was
colonized by Strongbow after the Anglo-Norman
invasion of 1170, and because of its central location
it was the venue of several Irish parliaments in the
fourteenth to sixteenth centuries. The Statutes of
Kilkenny were introduced here in 1366, and in 1642
the town was the meeting place of the Confederate
Catholics who surrendered to Cromwell in 1650.

LAOIS

Badge: Two gold lions passant gardant on a
red ground, over two gold fleur-de-lys on a
blue ground
Gaelic: *Laoighis* (Land of warriors or heroes)

Originally known as Queen's County, founded in
the late seventeenth century, it was also known by
the anglicized name of Leix, hence the market
town of Abbeyleix. Its chief town was originally
called Maryborough, after Queen Mary, the wife of
William of Orange, but like the country name, this
was dropped when southern Ireland attained a
measure of independence in 1922 and the name
Port Laoise (the port of Leix) was adopted instead.
A mainly agricultural district, its impressive ruins
testify to its turbulent history, exemplified by the
castle of the Fitzgeralds (1250), sacked by the
Scots (1315), rebuilt by the English, and
demolished by Cromwell's soldiers (1650).

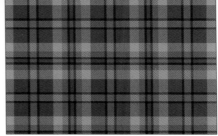

LIMERICK

Badge: A gold cross pattee in a gold circle
on three vertical wavy white lines on a
green ground
Gaelic: *Luimneach*

This county takes its name from the port of Limerick,
which was one of the chief towns of the ancient
province of Munster, and has been identified with the
Regia of the Roman cartographer Ptolemy. It is
believed to have been Christianized by St. Patrick,
but the earliest record of the town occurs in 812
when it was sacked by the Danes, who subsequently
made it their capital. After Contarf (1014), it was the
seat of Brian Boroimhe, High King of Ireland, whose
descendants, the O'Briens, reigned as kings of
Thomond (North Munster) from 1106 until it was
conquered by the English in 1174. The original Gaelic
name was Aine-Cliach, but the modern name is
derived from Hlymrekr, a Viking name.

LONDONDERRY

Badge: Two wheat sheaves flanking a white
rose over a red hand
Gaelic: *Doire* (Oak wood)

Most northwesterly of the six counties of Northern
Ireland, it was traditionally known as Derry, from a
sixth century monastery called Doire Calgaich
(Calgach's oak wood). The surrounding land was
inhabited by the O'Carhans, who owed allegiance
to the O'Neills. This land was subjugated in the
1580s and renamed Coleraine, after the town that
became the county seat. In 1609, the O'Neills were
forfeited and their chief towns given to the City of
London, which is how both the town and county of
Derry came to be known as Londonderry. It was at
Dungiven in this county that the earliest authentic
piece of tartan was discovered in a peat bog,
which later gave rise to the Ulster tartan.

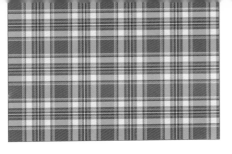

MANX LAXEY RED

Badge: Three legs, joined, booted, and
spurred, with the Latin motto *Quocunque
jeceris (gesseris) stabit* (Whichever way
you throw it, it will stand)
Gaelic: *Eilean Mhannan* (Ellan Vannin)

The Isle of Man was colonized by the Goidelic Celts
at the beginning of the Christian era, and the Manx
have a language akin to Scots and Irish but spelled
phonetically. Although the last native speaker died
in 1974, there has been a tremendous resurgence
of interest in all aspects of Manx culture and the
language is now actively promoted. From the
eighth until the thirteenth centuries, the island
formed part of the Hiberno-Norse empire and this
is reflected in many of its place-names to this day.
Laxey (Salmon Island) is the home of the Great
Wheel of the Lady Isabella lead mine, one of the
island's main tourist attractions today.

MANX NATIONAL

The Isle of Man was passed to Scotland under the
treaty that followed the defeat of Haakon V of
Norway at Largs in 1263, but in the 1290s it fell into
the hands of Edward I of England, who granted the
title of Lord of Man to the Stanley family, later Earls
of Derby. The marriage of the Derby heiress to
John, second Duke of Atholl, in 1736 brought the
island into the hands of the Murray family. The third
duke sold his rights to the Crown in 1765 and
today Queen Elizabeth is Lord (not Lady) of Man.
Nevertheless, the ancient rights of the Manx were
preserved, including their laws and Tynwald, the
world's oldest democratic assembly with a
continuous history, dating from 979. The
millennium of this ancient body was marked by the
creation of a number of tartans, either alluding to
specific features of the island or all-purpose setts
such as the national tartan.

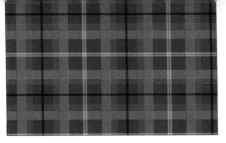

MAYO

Badge: A white saltire cross on a red
ground, bearing five crosses, with a castle
at the top and green trees at the sides,
and crossed battle-axes in the upper left
quadrant
Gaelic: *Maigh Eo* (Salmon plain or field)

This county of Connaught bounded on the north and
west by the Atlantic is the third largest in Ireland, yet
it takes its name from a hamlet near Claremorris, the
site of a seventh-century monastery founded by St.
Colman and later the seat of a bishopric. This district
was colonized by the Firbolgs at the beginning of the
Christian era and it was at Cong (famous for its wheel
cross) that they were annihilated. Later the territory
was ruled by the MacWilliam clan, descendants of
William de Burgh, a powerful Norman magnate.
Familes called De Burca or Bourke are from the same
source, and Bourke is the name of the Earls of Mayo.

MEATH

Badge: A king, crowned and sceptred,
seated on a throne
Gaelic: *Midhe* (Modern *mee*, meaning "neck")

This was originally the name of a large area in the
province of Leinster, which incorporated not only
the present county but also Westmeath and
Longford as well as parts of Cavan, Kildare, and
Offaly. Meath was an independent kingdom by
130 under Tuathal, who owed allegiance to the
High King of Ireland. Kings of Meath continued until
1173, when Henry II granted the lordship to Hugh
de Lacy. Although a county was founded by
Edward I in 1296, this part of the country was not
fully subjugated until the 1540s. The most famous
site in Meath is the prehistoric mound and stone
circle constituting the Hill of Tara, the seat of the
High Kings of Ireland, which has its own tartan.

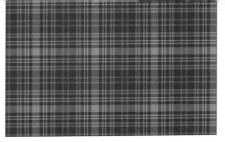 

O'BRIEN

Badge: Three lions passant gardant, half
  gold, half white, on a red ground
Gaelic: *Ui Briain*

The prefix Ui (anglicized as O') signifies the family or descendants of some common ancestor. In this case it denotes the descendants, kinsmen, or followers of the great Brian Boru (Boroimhe). Born around 926, he succeeded to the chieftainship of the Dál Cais in 976 and then became High King of All Ireland in 1002. Inevitably, this led to a showdown with the Vikings, whom he defeated decisively at Clontarf in 1014, but paid with his life. One of the most powerful families in Ireland, the O'Briens became Earls of Thomond and Inchiquin. Famous members of the clan include William Smith O'Brien, leader of the Young Ireland movement in the 1840s; the patriot William O'Brien (1852–1958); the statesman Conor Cruise O'Brien; and the novelist Edna O'Brien.

O'CONNOR

Badge: A green tree on a white ground
Gaelic: *Ui Conaire*

This great family stems from Conchobar (lover of hounds), who ruled Connaught in the tenth century. Among his descendants were the High Kings Turlough O'Connor (died 1156) and Rory O'Connor (died 1198), the last holder of that title. In more recent times, another Rory O'Connor was one of the patriots who fought the British to secure the independence of Ireland. One of the prominent Republicans captured by the Nationalists at the fall of the Four Courts in 1922, he was executed by a firing squad soon afterward. Other clan members include Feargus O'Connor (1794–1855), leader of the Chartist movement, which laid the foundations for the parliamentary democracy in effect today. In 1981, Sandra Day O'Connor became the first female justice of the U.S. Supreme Court.

O'NEILL

Badge: The red hand of Ulster flanked by
facing red lions rampant
Gaelic: *Ui Niall*

The third of Ireland's greatest families claims descent from Niall of the Nine Hostages, the son of a British slave who became King of Ireland (379–405) and fought campaigns against Britain and Gaul as well as his Irish rivals. One of his fourteen sons was Eoghan, from whom the O'Neills are directly descended. They split into northern and southern branches, although both provided many of the high kings. A scion of the northern branch was Colm (Columba), who Christianized the Picts. From Eoghan comes the name of the county Tyrone (Tir Eoghainn), and in time the O'Neills became the earls of Tyrone, many of whom played a prominent part in Irish history. The tartan shown here is one of three and is worn by the Shane O'Neill pipe band of New Jersey.

ROSCOMMON

Badge: A gold *V* enclosing a green field
bearing a gold cross pattee and crown,
flanked by a ram's head and a sprig of
shamrock proper on a blue ground
Gaelic: *Ros Comáin* (The wooded heights
of St. Coman)

Situated in eastern Connaught, Roscommon is in the center of Ireland and takes its name from the seventh-century cleric who founded a monastery where the county town now stands. The district was granted by Henry III to Richard de Burgh but remained in the hands of indigenous clans, including the McDermotts and McDonoughs, although the O'Connor family alone survived dispossession in the aftermath of Cromwell's campaign of 1649–50. The county contains the ruins of the ancient kings of Connaught at Crogan (Rathcroghan).

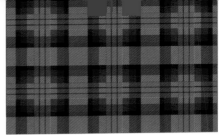

TARA (MURPHY)

Badge: Four lions rampant on alternate
red and white quarters, divided by a
horizontal black band bearing three
gold wheat sheaves
Gaelic: *Uí Mhurchú* (The family of Murdoch)

Tara in County Meath is the artificial hill, which in the
Middle Ages was the seat of the High Kings of Ireland
until suppressed by the English in the late twelfth
century. It was here that the sacred Stone of Destiny
(Lia Fáil) was used for coronations before it was
transferred to Iona and thence to Dunstaffnage and
Scone in the heart of Scotland. This tartan, however,
was published in *Clan Originaux* (1880), where it was
listed as being the sett of the Murphy family. One of
the commonest Irish surnames, it is borne by the
Australian choreographer Graeme, the statesman
Keith, as well as the American comic actor Eddie and
the hemotologist William Murphy (1892–1987).

TIPPERARY

Badge: On a field of ermine, a band
alternating blue, red, and gold bearing
two sets of three corbs
Gaelic: *Tiobraid Arann*

The sixth-largest county in Ireland, Tipperary forms
part of the province of Munster. The name is of
immense antiquity and dates back to the fifth
century, if not earlier, when it was converted to
Christianity by St. Patrick himself. It lies in the heart
of the finest dairy-farming country and is renowned
for its cheese, butter, and (more recently)
condensed milk products. The county was founded
by King John in 1210 and for centuries it was
largely in the possession of the Butler family, Earls
and, later, Dukes of Ormonde. Tipperary is one of
the best-known Irish names, largely on account of
Jack Judge's popular marching song of the British
Army in World War I, *It's a Long Way to Tipperary*.

TYRONE

Badge: The red hand of Ulster on a white
　　ground surmounted by a blue band
　　bearing a fleur-de-lys
Gaelic: *Tir Eoghainn* (The land of Eoghan)

This county of Northern Ireland derives its name from Eoghan, one of the sons of Niall of the Nine Hostages in the fifth century, from whom were descended the Ui Niall (Hy Neill) and their numerous septs. The chief seat of this powerful family was at Dungannon and in the reign of Henry VIII, the earldom of Tyrone was conferred on Conn O'Neill. A dispute over the succession to the title led to the uprising led by Shane O'Neill (the people's choice), killed in battle in 1567. In the civil wars of the 1640s, Sir Phelim O'Neill and Owen Roe O'Neill were often victorious over Parliamentary forces, and Tyrone was one of the last counties to hold out for James II in 1690. Tyrone was for many years a center for coal and textile industries.

ULSTER

Badge: A red cross on a gold field, with
　　a white shield bearing the red hand at
　　the center
Gaelic: *Uladh*

Ulster is one of the four historic provinces of Ireland. By 400 it had been divided into three petty kingdoms: Oriel (Oirghialla) in the south, Aileach (Tyrone), and Ulidia (Antrim and Down). In the Middle Ages the Ui Niall were the dominant clan and later the O'Neills and O'Donnells were the most prominent families. After the flight of the indigenous earls in 1607, King James VI and I introduced English and Scottish settlers. The Ulster tartan is based on a pair of trews unearthed from a bog by William Dixon, farmer of "The Hill," Flanders Townland near Dungiven. It dates to the beginning of the seventeenth century. The cloth had a green check but was stained reddish-brown by peat.

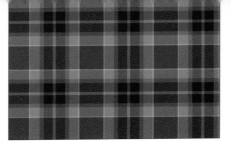 

WATERFORD

Badge: A vertical column of three vessels
with furled sails on stylized waves
Gaelic: *Port Láirge* (Thigh port)

The most easterly county of Munster, it derives its
name from the county town, which in turn was
anciently known as Menapia and, later, Cuan na
Groith (harbor of the sun). It was an important
stronghold of the Danes from 914 until 1171, when
they were driven out by Strongbow. Its modern
English name comes from the Norse *Vatnafjordur*.
The curious Irish name comes from the fancied
resemblance of the harbor to the shape of a
thighbone. It has important ecclesiastical
connections; the cathedral at Ardmore was
erected on the site of the monastery founded by
St. Declan in the seventh century. Today it is
renowned all over the world for its glassware,
Waterford crystal.

WESTMEATH

Badge: A saltire divided into blue (top and
bottom) or red (sides), bearing a gold ring
supported by gold lions rampant, with a
swan above and a horned helmet below
Gaelic: *Iar Midhe*

The ancient fifth province of Ireland known as Meath
was broken up in 1543 and it was at that time that
the county of Westmeath was formed and attached
to Leinster. Situated in the center of the island,
much of its surface is covered with bogs and lakes,
but it also boasts several hills. Although none of
them is of any great eminence, it is said that at least
a score of the thirty-two counties can be seen on a
clear day from the 800-foot summit of Knocklaydey.
Westmeath is mainly an agricultural county, but its
historic and ecclesiastical connections, together
with its abundance of brown trout, attract visitors
from every part of the world.

WEXFORD

Badge: Three lymphads (galleys) on a white
   ground
Gaelic: *Loch Garman*

This county of Leinster lies on the Irish shore of St. George's Channel and its port of Rosslare, developed in 1906, is now one of the principal terminals for ferries operating from England and France to Ireland. Hy Kinselagh, the northern part of the county, was the territory of the Mac Murroughs, overlords of Leinster, but it was overrun in the ninth century by the Danes, who gave the name of Vacasfjordur; the ruins of their encampments are very numerous, but they were driven out by the Anglo-Norman FitzStephen in 1169. It was named a county by King John, who granted it to William Marshal, Earl of Pembroke, although it later fell into the hands of the Talbot Earls of Shrewsbury. Wexford was the center of the uprising led by Wolfe Tone in 1798.

WICKLOW

Badge: A gold lion on a blue field over a
   Celtic church on a green field
Gaelic: *Cill Mhantáin*

This county of Leinster lies to the south of Dublin and is bounded by St. George's Channel and the counties of Wexford, Carlow, and Kildare. The county, which was not founded until 1606, takes its name from the seaport that was known to the Vikings as Vikingaló. The Gaelic name, however, alludes to the cell of the hermit St. Mantan, who was associated with St. Kevin in the early seventh century. Gold was at one time mined in the Wicklow Mountains around Croghan Kinshela, while copper, lead, and sulphur have also been discovered in commercial quantities. Today tourism is the major industry, and visitors are drawn from every part of the globe to Glendalough (the valley of the two lakes) and the beautiful Vale of Avoca.

Index